CELTIC
BACKSTITCH

CELTIC BACKSTITCH

Helen Hall

Guild of Master Craftsman Publications Ltd

First published 2004 by
Guild of Master Craftsman Publications Ltd,
166 High Street, Lewes,
East Sussex, BN7 1XN

ISBN 1 86108 368 8

The publisher and author can accept no legal responsibility for
any consequences arising from the application of information, advice
or instructions given in this publication.

Please note: Thread colour codes refer to the threads used in the projects as shown in the
photographs. The charts and keys should be regarded as reference only.
The average completion times given are based on a stitcher of average ability
stitching for two hours a day.

A catalogue record of this book is available from the British Library.

Publisher: Paul Richardson
Art Director: Ian Smith
Production Manager: Stuart Poole
Managing Editor: Gerrie Purcell
Commissioning Editor: April McCroskie
Editor: Clare Miller
Designer: John Hawkins

Typefaces: Hiroshige Book and ITC Kallos
Colour origination by MRM Graphics
Printed and bound by Kyodo, Singapore

Contents

Introduction

Part One Tools and Materials

Part Two Projects

Introduction

In putting this book together I wanted to celebrate the huge variety of Celtic art that exists. Most of us are very aware of the more commonly used and extremely popular knotwork patterns, whether it is in its most simplistic form or shown in designs so complex that it is difficult to follow the network of 'ribbons' as they pass under and over each other, twisting this way and that as they go. A lot of people will also recognize the key pattern designs; these patterns are very often like mazes, using straight lines in many different positions to fill an empty space, but still allowing free passage between these lines from one point to another. Then there are the zoomorphic designs, which are essentially another form of knotwork, but with a lot of features from animals incorporated to give them a whole new dimension and a very different look. Spirals, triskeles and whirligigs are also quite commonplace. Sometimes these are used on their own, but more often they are used in conjunction with other patterns, especially knotwork.

I have included several examples of these types of designs, not as a direct copy of existing designs, but showing my own interpretation of them or simply using the same sort of techniques put together in my own style. However, I also wanted to include a few patterns which are examples of some of the lesser known types of Celtic designs, many of these dating from as early as the 5th/4th centuries BC and are often used to decorate pottery, metalwork and jewellery. A lot of these designs are very reminiscent of artwork accredited to other, so-called more civilized cultures, such as the Romans and the Greeks, but no one really knows who developed them first. As the Celts were fairly widespread, at one time or another inhabiting most parts of Europe, and extremely accomplished artisans, working in many different mediums, who's to say if they developed these designs themselves or simply copied them because they were popular with the people with whom they traded.

One thing is for certain, these designs were most commonplace prior to the Celts being driven out of most of mainland Europe, which does suggest that they may have been derived from the influences of other cultures. Once they were in a more isolated climate, their artwork developed into the very distinctive style that is so easily recognizable as Celtic.

When working these designs don't be put off a particular design by my choice of fabric or thread colours; don't be afraid to change them if you prefer something different. I have chosen the colourways I have used simply to show a range of different combinations. The beauty of using this type of stitching and these designs is that there is no right or wrong colour combinations. If it works for you, then it works!

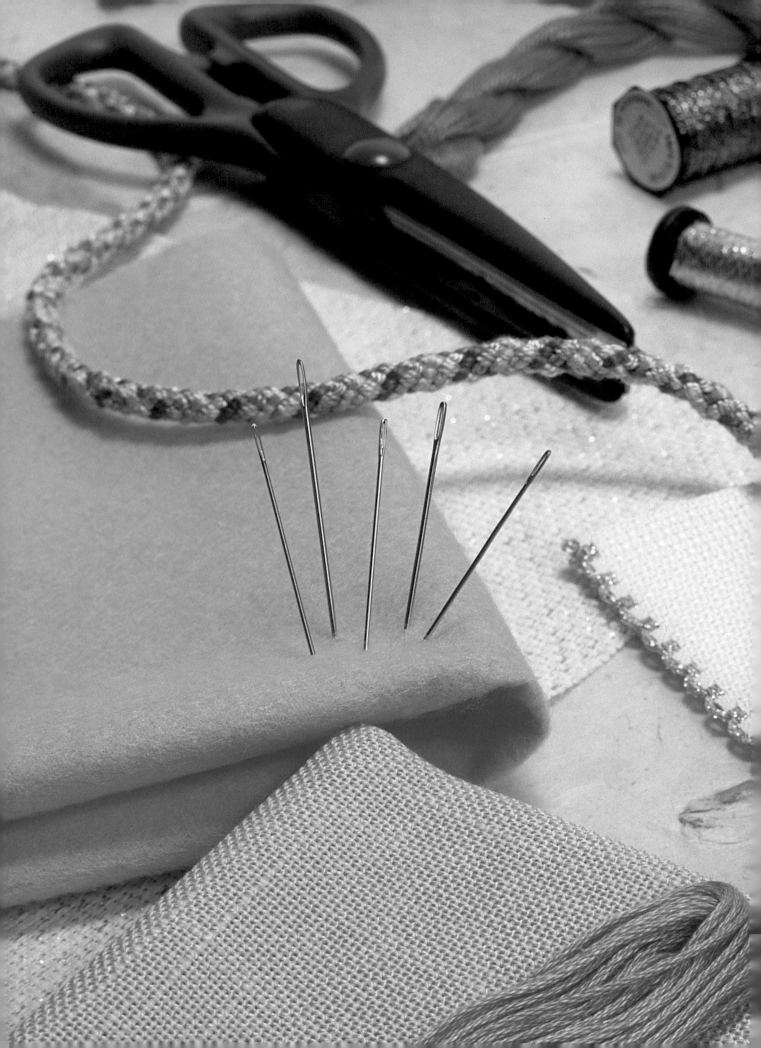

Part One

Tools and Materials

This section deals with the tools, materials and techniques that I have used for the projects in this book, including any specialist items that you may not have readily to hand. It also outlines alternative materials that you could use in order to add those little personal touches that will make your projects more individual.

Chapter one

Working the designs

Fig 1.1
A selection of
needlework
fabrics

Fabrics

Needlework that requires an even spacing of stitches (known as counted thread-work) should be carried out on fabrics with even weave, that is, fabrics that have an equal number of evenly spaced warp (vertical) threads and weft (horizontal) threads. Such fabrics are usually referred to by their count; that is the number of threads that can be counted, in either direction, to the square inch/centimetre. Aida is a type of evenweave fabric, often described as a blockweave because of its appearance. As with all evenweave fabrics, Aida has the same number of threads in each direction, but they are woven into blocks, which creates clearly visible holes. This manner of weaving makes the fabric quite stiff and is, therefore, less prone to distortion unlike some of the other softer evenweave fabrics, such as linen. With Aida, the count refers to the number of holes in each direction, rather than the number of threads which is the way in which the softer linen-type fabrics are defined.

My choice

I have used 14-count Aida for all the designs as it tends to be the most readily available fabric and is the easiest to work with, especially if you are a beginner. However, if you prefer to work on a different count, there is no reason why you shouldn't, but remember that the higher the count the smaller the finished design will be and, likewise, the lower the count the larger it will be. You can also replace Aida with any other type of evenweave fabrics, but remember that the looser weave of some of these fabrics can lead to distortion so try not to pull your stitches too tight or you could ruin your finished piece.

Fig 1.2
14-count Aida

Threads

There are many different types of thread available nowadays, making needlework in all its forms a very popular hobby and much cheaper too than it was when only finely spun silk was available. The variety of threads also helps today's stitcher to achieve all sorts of different effects.

Stranded cotton floss

This is the most popular choice for ordinary types of counted threadwork. It is a very versatile type of thread that can be used in different thicknesses for different effects. It can also be used for both embroidery-type stitching and general stitching in situations where there is not too much stress put on it. It also comes in a spectacular range of colours, with new colours being added all the time so you are sure to find the colours you want. Usually, it is available in a six-stranded form

Fig 1.3 Stranded cotton floss

and when cut into suitable lengths, preferably about 16in (40cm) long, you can separate the strands into whatever number you require for the effect you want without too great a chance of getting it knotted.

Metallic embroidery thread and cord

Stranded metallic embroidery thread is useful to add a little sparkle to a design, but its colour range tends to be somewhat limited. Also, it is very fine, so to achieve your desired thickness you will need a greater number of strands than with ordinary cotton floss or metallic cord. However, these threads are quite slippery so it can be difficult to keep your needle threaded while you work. In addition to this, the metallic surface of both the thread and the cord can be damaged quite easily so you do need to take extra care when working with them.

Fig 1.4 Metallic embroidery cord

Stitching note

Instead of working solely in metallic threads, try combining one strand of ordinary cotton floss with one or two strands of metallic thread. This way you can achieve a subtle glitter effect without it completely dominating the design and the cotton floss will help to protect the metallic surface. Try out different combinations of colours and thread types; a darker or lighter shade of cotton floss will make the metallic thread stand out while a contrasting colour will add a more dramatic effect. For a shimmery effect rather than a glittery one use rayon thread instead of metallic thread. Rayon thread can also be blended with cotton floss for a more subtle look.

Some manufacturers produce spools of metallic blending threads which are specifically intended for use with cotton floss or other non-metallic threads. Spools of ready-blended metallic cord, where many threads are twisted or woven together to make a corded effect, are also available. These also come in different thicknesses (the finest of which can be used with other threads) and an ever-improving selection of colours. When working these types of backstitch designs, it is best to use a fine cord on its own or very fine cord if you want to add a strand of cotton floss to it. Otherwise you will lose the pattern definition in the more intricate of your designs.

Perlé cotton

Perlé cotton is a two-ply thread not a stranded one and so consequently should not be split. Perlé has a more lustrous look to it than ordinary stranded cotton floss and, although not available in all the colours that cotton floss comes in, it does have a pretty good range. It comes in a number of different thicknesses and, again, for this type of stitching, choose a fine thread, especially when working more detailed designs.

Fig 1.5 Perlé cotton

Fig 1.6 Variegated threads

Variegated threads

Many manufacturers now offer quite a good range of variegated or 'space-dyed' threads in a number of their different thread types. These work extremely well with the type of stitching used in this book as the colour fades in and out gently as the pattern is worked.

Fig 1.7 Gold metallic cord is used in the pieces in Chapter 10 to contrast with the green in the design

My choice

I have used six-stranded cotton floss alone for almost all of the designs in this book because of its excellent colour range, availability and reasonable price. However, in Chapter 10 I have used gold metallic cord to bring out the depth of colour in the Christmas green for the cushion cover and curtain tie-backs.

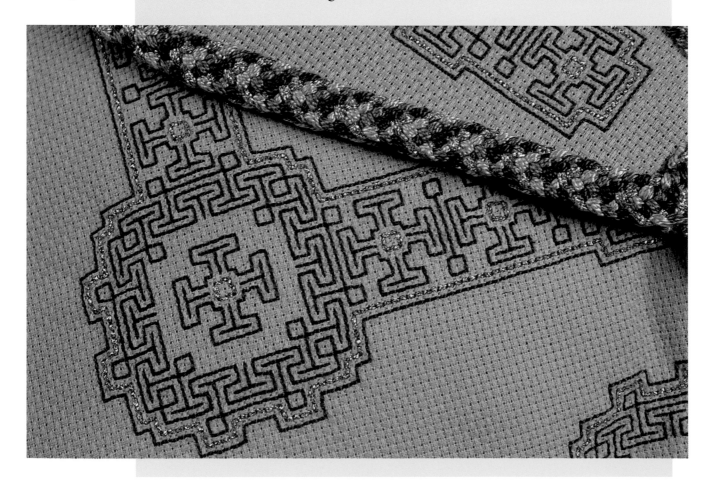

EQUIPMENT

This section provides a list of the equipment you will need to start stitching the projects in this book. Some of this equipment you will need for all the projects and some you will only need for a few of them.

Needles

To stitch the actual designs you need a blunt tapestry needle, size 24 or 26. The blunt 'point' of these needles is intended to make it easier to stitch cleanly through the holes of the fabric without splitting the threads, which would result in uneven stitches and spoil your work.

You will also need a sharp sewing needle to stitch up some of the projects. However, you can use a tapestry needle when stitching two layers of Aida together by matching the holes.

Fig 1.8 Sewing and tapestry needles

Sewing machine

This is not an essential item as all the projects in this book can be made up by hand-sewing the seams; however, using a sewing machine can cut down on the time it takes to complete these stages of the making-up process. It is essential though, that you are very careful when using a sewing machine that you do not let it run away with you as the bulk of the layers of fabric in some of the projects can cause the stitching to wander and it is harder to unpick machine stitching on Aida, ribbons and so forth without damaging them than it is on plain cotton fabrics.

Scissors

You need two pairs of scissors, a pair of fabric shears or dressmaking scissors, which you will need solely for cutting the various fabrics to size, and also a pair of small, sharp-pointed embroidery scissors which you will use for cutting and trimming the threads and for trimming back some amounts of fabric. The pointed ends of these scissors are also useful for unpicking your work should you happen to make a mistake. However, if you do have to use them for this purpose, be very careful not to cut the strands of the fabric as well. It will help to place your needle under the stitch you want to cut and lift it away from the fabric a little so that you can slide the point of the scissors under the thread cleanly before you cut. Please remember that if you want to keep your embroidery scissors sharp it is important to use them only for cutting threads and trimming small areas of fabric. If you do use them for cutting other items (particularly paper), you will find they will quickly become blunt and will no longer cut through thread cleanly, which can lead to all sorts of problems.

Fig 1.9 Choose a pair of fabric shears (centre) or dressmaking scissors (far right) for cutting fabric to size and a smaller pair of scissors for trimming and unpicking

Frame

The use of a frame is a matter of personal preference, but you will find it useful for many of the projects in this book, as it would be impossible to keep the tension correct while working over such large areas.

I use a rolling frame as I have found this type of frame most suited to this type of stitching particularly when working on big projects. These are rectangular frames with straight, solid side struts and rollers top and bottom. You pin or tack your fabric to these strips of fabric webbing attached to the rollers, then you simply turn them in opposite directions to take up the slack in the fabric until it is stretched tight between them and lock them in place by tightening the fastenings. Rolling frames are available in various widths so it is easy to get one to suit whichever project you want to stitch. They are also quite reasonably priced, so if you are a keen stitcher, it might pay to invest in more than one frame in order to give yourself a selection of widths. I have several frames ranging from 12in (30cm) wide up to 24in (60cm) so that I can use the width most suited to the size of project that I am stitching at the time.

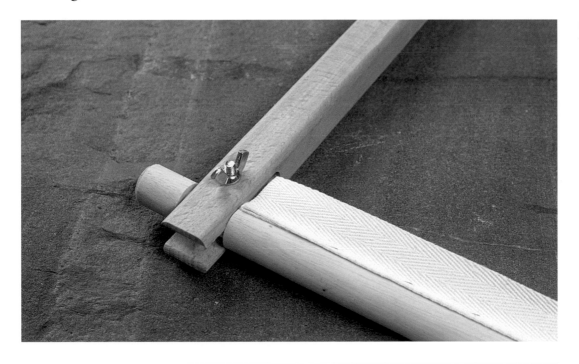

Fig 1.10 Rolling frames are particularly useful for bigger projects

Tacking your fabric to the rollers is the correct way to attach it and the extra time this takes to do will be worth it in the long run; however, I do sometimes use pins myself when working a design that I know will not take me too long. It is useful to note that if you do pin your fabric to the frame, you really must not leave it stretched tight for long periods of time or the pinheads will distort the shape of the fabric. You will also need to check the rollers regularly to be sure that none of your pins have come loose or dropped out. If they do fall out the tension will be altered, and you will also run the risk of having the painful experience of treading on one.

MAKING UP THE FINISHED PIECE

When you have finished stitching the design and you are sure that it is clean, dry and the right shape, it is time to make up the finished article. Specific instructions for making up each individual project are given at the end of each chapter, but I have listed here all the extra items that you will need for the various projects that you may not have readily to hand. That way you can collect together everything you need before you start the final process, which will save you time and avoid unnecessary frustration.

MATERIALS

Felt

Felt is made from pressed wool, it is a multi-purpose, non-fraying fabric and comes in a good range of colours. I use felt on projects where I need just a little bit of padding to disguise any little lumps or bumps in my work, where even the lightest weight of wadding would be too thick. I also use it as a backing material when I want to hide the stitching on the reverse side of a finished item. Because of the good selection of colours available you can match, complement or contrast the backing of your finished piece with the Aida or thread you have used.

Fig 1.11 Felt can be bought in a range of colours

Baize can also be used in the same way, but as it lacks the colour range and thickness of felt it is not so useful and I would only use it in a situation where I could not get hold of any suitable felt.

Interfacing

Interfacing comes in different weights (light, medium and heavy) and in iron-on or stitch-on varieties. I use medium-weight iron-on interfacing on small projects such as coasters where small amounts of fabric need to be trimmed to fit into a limited space. It prevents fabrics from fraying and stiffens them too, which can be useful in lots of situations.

Fig 1.12 Using iron-on interfacing prevents fabric from fraying

Fig 1.13 Use hemming webbing and bonding sheets to fuse pieces of fabric together

Hemming webbing and bonding sheets

Iron-on hemming webbing is a mesh-like tape that is used to bond two layers of fabric together, usually hems, hence the name. A similar material, Bond-a-Web, is available in sheet form; this is useful for fusing larger pieces of fabric together. I use both forms in place of glue for fixing felt to the reverse side of an item and other fabrics to the felt where I need a lining.

Braid

All the braid shown in this book I make myself so that I can match the colours used to particular projects. However, as there is a good range of manufactured braiding available these days you do not need to go to such lengths yourself. You could even use ribbon instead if you are not able to find a suitable braid. I use braid for finishing off projects, sometimes to cover raw edges and sometimes simply for decorative purposes.

Fig 1.14
Round braid

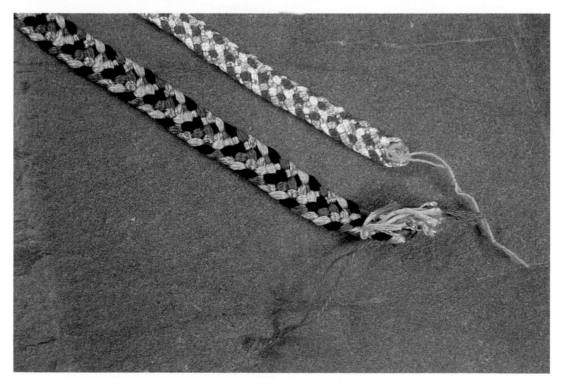

Fig 1.15
Flat braid

Fig 1.16
Rounded flat braid

Fig 1.17
You can use ribbon if no suitable braid is available

If you think you would like to try making your own braid, I would recommend *Beginner's Guide to Braiding: The Craft of Kumihimo* by Jacqui Catley (Search Press), which provides all the necessary information you need to get started with Japanese braiding, or, for the slightly more advanced, *Making Kumihimo* by Rodrick Owen (GMC Publications). However, you should be aware that you will need some specialist equipment to do it.

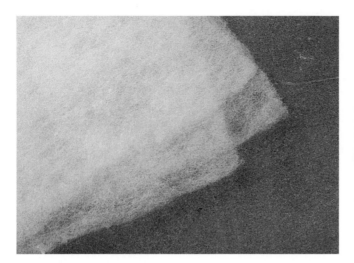

Wadding and filling

Wadding is another item that comes in different weights. In its flat form it is ideal to pad out designs to help disguise any little lumps or bumps that may have developed during the stitching process without you realizing it. This often happens on projects where you need to change colours a lot, so you are continually starting and fastening off threads in the same area. Lightweight polyester wadding is the most suitable for this purpose as it is thick enough to disguise the lumps, but not so thick that it makes the finished item too bulky.

The best way to stuff cushion covers, in my opinion, is with ready-made cushion inserts, as this will make life so much easier when you want to wash them. They also come in a range of sizes so it is fairly easy to find the right one for your cover. However, if you prefer, there is nothing stopping you making your own insert or simply stuffing the cover with filling. Make sure that you use flame-retardant, polyester fillings though, to minimize the risk of fire.

Fabric stiffener

This is a safe, non-toxic liquid which stops fabrics fraying beyond the point that it is applied to. It is best applied with a small paintbrush, like those found in children's paint sets. When fabric stiffener dries, it acts like a glue and sticks the

Fig 1.18
Above left:
Wadding can be used to disguise lumps and bumps in fabric

Fig 1.19
Above right:
Use fabric stiffener to stop fraying

threads of the fabric together, so it is unable to fray. I use it where there is no room for a hem and in other situations such as when I am making a fringed edge, as for the table mat and bookmarks in this book.

Lavender

Lavender is my favourite pot-pourri and has been all my life, together with old-fashioned roses. I grow my own lavender, so it is easy for me to harvest and dry it and I always try to have a small supply put by, especially for the winter months. However, scents are a very personal choice so there is no reason why you should not substitute lavender for your own favourite pot-pourri as long as it is a dry mix. Never use a wet/damp mix as this will cause the fabric to become mouldy and ruin your work. Try out different combinations depending on the time of year or, if the item is intended to be a present to someone, fill it with their favourite pot-pourri mix.

Fig 1.20
Dried lavender

If you want to try drying lavender yourself, here are a few tips:

- Do not cut lavender when the flowers are wet or they will go mouldy before they have a chance to dry out

- Try to cut the stem as long as possible as this makes it easier to tie the stems in bunches

- Tie the stems into small bunches: if the bunch is too big air may not be able to circulate around the central flowers. If any of the flowers aren't dry they could start to go mouldy and the whole bunch will be ruined

- Hang these upside down in a warm, dry place (ideally an airing cupboard or somewhere similar): if you tried to hang the bunch from the flowers, a very difficult task, the bunch would fall as the dried flowerheads came away from the stalk

- Secure a paper bag around the flower heads as individual flowers may fall off during the drying process; this creates a mess and leaves the flowers unusable

- In these conditions, it normally takes about two weeks for the flowers to dry. It is easy to check if they are ready; simply remove the bag and rub your finger and thumb down the flower spike, against the direction of the growth. If the individual flowers feel hard and crisp and come away from the stem easily, the drying process is complete; if not, replace the bag and hang the bunch up for another few days

- To harvest the flowers, follow the same procedure as when testing for dryness. Store them in an air-tight container, away from direct sunlight, to preserve their scent.

Chapter two
Techniques

GETTING STARTED

The first thing you have to do is cut your Aida to size. This type of fabric is easy to cut in a straight line as you can simply follow a line of holes. The size of Aida required is given at the start of each project.

Finding the centre

Once you have cut your Aida to size you need to find the centre as this is where you will start from. Counted threadwork is always stitched from the centre of the fabric outwards as there are no guidelines or patterns printed on the fabric for you to follow and it is important to be sure that the design will be central to the fabric when it is completed. To find the centre, fold the fabric in half in one direction, then in half again in the other direction; the hole at the point where the folds cross is the centre.

Fig 2.1 Fold the fabric vertically then horizontally to find the centre

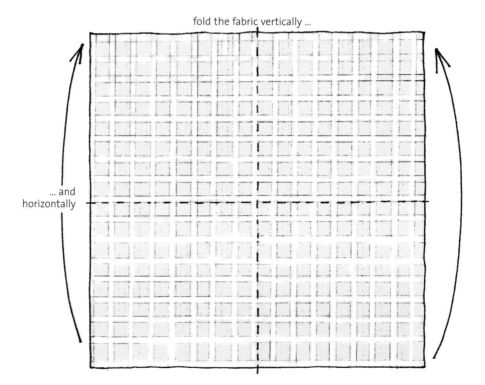

Adjustments for central blocks

If you find that you have a block at the centre point instead of a hole, don't worry, simply move to one of the four holes surrounding it, it doesn't matter particularly which one. However, you will probably need to trim a line of blocks from one side of the design when you have finished to even up the distance between the design and the edges once you have finished the stitching.

It is a good idea to mark the centre so that you don't lose your place before you even start stitching. If the design is small and you are ready to start straight away, simply slip a pin into the hole. However, if the design is a large and repetitive one, like the Hippi bag, it is a good idea to mark it in a more permanent and obvious way. Tie a large knot at one end of a good length of brightly coloured, fairly thick thread, but make sure that it isn't a colour you'll be using in the design. Thread a

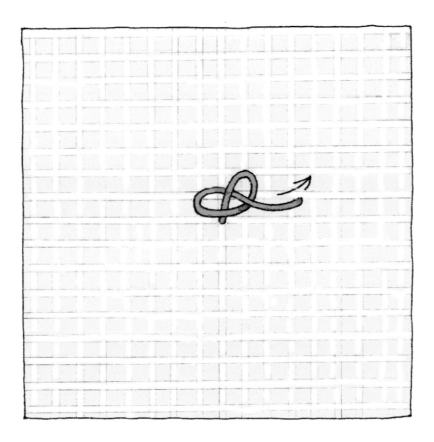

Fig 2.2 Mark the centre of large designs with thread

needle with this and draw it through the centre hole; the length of thread will now be on the right side of the Aida. Tie a small bow in it so that you will not be able to pull it out by mistake, this marks the centre of your design and you can simply move it to one side when you need to stitch into the centre hole. When you have finished stitching or if you want to remove the thread before then, simply untie or cut the bow off and pull the thread out from the back of the fabric. It is important that you avoid stitching through your marker thread or you won't be able to remove it when the time comes.

To find the centre of the graph draw a line lightly with a pencil on the paper (or just visualize the line) to join the top and bottom arrows and another to join the side arrows – where these two lines cross is the centre. If there is no stitch at the centre of the design, count outwards from that point to the first stitch shown on the graph, in whichever direction that might be, then mirror your actions on the Aida. This will be your starting point.

STARTING AND FINISHING THREADS

It is important to avoid using knots to start or finish a thread as they create lumps in your work which will spoil the look of the finished item. To start off the first thread insert your needle from the back of the fabric and draw the thread through, leaving about ¾in (2cm) on the reverse side. Hold this 'tail' against the fabric and work a few stitches of the design over it.

Once you are sure it is secure, continue stitching until you have about 2in (5cm) of thread left in your needle. At this point, push the needle through to the back of the fabric and turn your work over. Weave your needle through the last few stitches you worked to secure the thread, then remove the needle and trim back any excess. It is important to trim back excess thread, especially when using dark

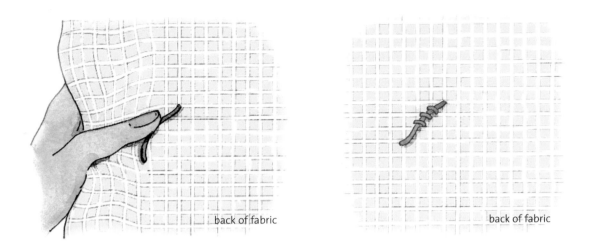

back of fabric

back of fabric

Fig 2.3 (Far left)
Hold the 'tail' flat
on the fabric to
start a thread

Fig 2.4 (Left)
Secure it by
working a few
stitches over it

Fig 2.5 (Below
left) To fasten off,
weave your
needle through
the last few
stitches at the
back of the
design

Fig 2.6 (Below
right) To work
one backstitch
bring your needle
up at 1, take it
down at 2, then
up again at 3

colours on light-coloured Aida, as they might show through to the front and spoil your design. However, do not cut the thread back too closely or it might work its way loose as you work other areas of the design.

Start and finish all threads in the same way as you finished off the first one, but try not to start and finish too many threads in the same area as this will create lumps in your work in the same way as a knot would.

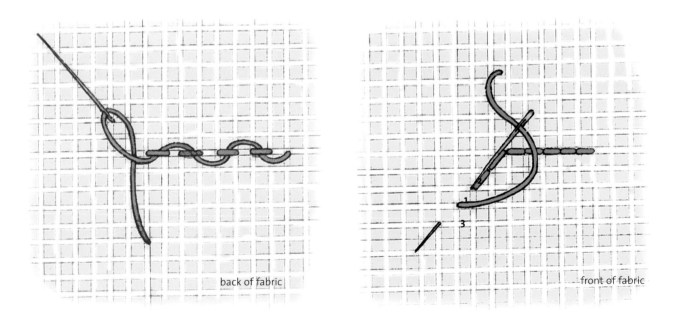

back of fabric

front of fabric

BACKSTITCH

The only stitch used in the designs in this book is backstitch. One stitch on the graph represents one block on the fabric, the distance between each hole. Backstitch is quick and easy to do, even for a complete beginner.

WASHING AND PRESSING YOUR WORK

You should always try to work with clean hands and avoid any situation where your work could be spoilt by dirt or spillages. However, if you have been working on a project for a long time it can become dirty, especially if it is light in colour. Ideally, you should try to store your work in a bag to protect it from general dirt, spillages and abrasive damage when you are not actually working on it.

If your work has become dirty then you will need to wash it. Handwash the item in lukewarm water with a small amount of mild hand-soap. Never wash your work in a washing machine and never use detergents as these are quite harsh; many detergents are either acidic or alkaline and will eat into the fabric. Never scrub the fabric either as this will damage the stitching and the surface of the fabric too. It is also important not to have the water too hot or the colours may run. However, if this does happen, don't panic, just keep rinsing the item in cold water until the water runs clear and the runs have disappeared.

After washing, always rinse your work thoroughly to remove all traces of the soap. If any soap remains it may eventually eat into the fabric, as soap very rarely has a neutral pH value. When you are satisfied that it is clean and soap-free, gently squeeze out all the excess water, and then roll the piece up in a clean towel. Squeeze the towel to remove as much of the remaining water as you can. It is OK to twist the towel gently as you are doing this, then unroll it and reshape the fabric as necessary.

Fold a clean, dry towel and place it on your ironing board. Lay your work face down on top of this and then carefully finish the drying with a medium-hot iron. Dab the iron onto the fabric rather than dragging it over the surface as this can cause distortion, continue until your piece is completely dry. You should press your work using this method even if you haven't had to wash it. It is also a good idea to leave it to 'air' in a warm, dry environment for a couple of hours afterwards to be absolutely certain that it is dry. If it is a big piece it might be advisable to leave it overnight.

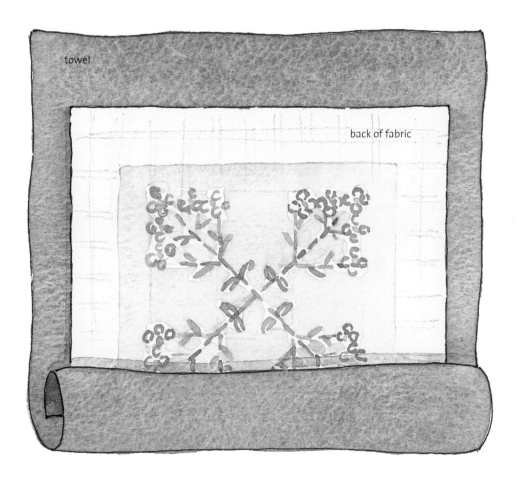

towel

back of fabric

Fig 2.7 Roll your work up in a towel and squeeze it gently to remove excess water

MAKING A TASSEL

You will need a 6–8in (15–20cm) length of suitably coloured cotton floss for each tassel you want to make; do not separate the strands but use it as it comes out of the skein. If you are making your tassel at the point where two lengths of braid meet you will need to wind the cotton floss tightly around the two loose ends of the braid as close to the fabric of the item as possible. Make sure that you cover the end you started with as you wind it so that it can't come loose and unravel.

When you have securely bound the braids together, thread a tapestry needle with the remaining end of the cotton floss and pass this under the thread you have just wound around the braid (the 'binding') on the reverse side of your work and pull it tight. Repeat this process several times to ensure that the thread can't work loose, then cut off any excess thread as close to the binding as possible.

Fig 2.8 Securing the end of a tassel

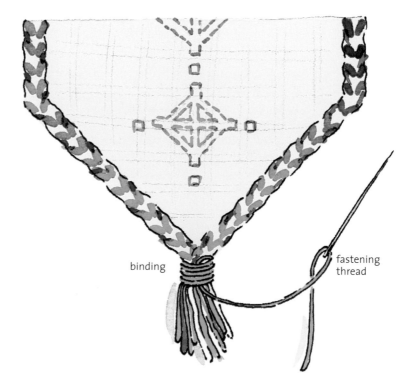

binding

fastening thread

If you are making your tassel as a form of finishing of one or more lengths of braid, as with the Hippi bag, simply start the binding as close as possible to the point where you finished stitching the braid to the fabric.

To form the 'tail' of the tassel, unravel the braiding that extends below the binding. The ends of the thread that form the tail are usually several different lengths. To make them neat and even wrap a piece of stiff paper tightly around them as close to the binding as possible, then slide it downwards until the bottom edge is level with the end of the shortest of the threads. Using your embroidery scissors, carefully trim off all the ends of the threads that protrude beyond this point. When you are satisfied that all the threads are the same length remove the paper and give the tassel a little shake to let it fall into place naturally.

You will probably find that the threads of the tail are a little curly from the time they have spent in the braid, similar to hair which has been plaited. If you would prefer them straighter try steaming them over the spout of a boiling kettle or pan of boiling water, then pull them straight. This process should be done before trimming the tail level. Do be careful not to scald yourself while doing this and never let children attempt to do it. Never hold your hands directly over the steam, hold the tassel so that it is only the tail that is over it. If you do get a slight scald hold it under cold water until the stinging subsides. In the case of a serious scald always seek medical advice.

Part Two

Projects

Choosing the projects for this book
was a very difficult task indeed as
I wanted to offer a selection that
would give a variety of styles,
complexity and ease-of-working.
I hope that I have achieved my goal.

Chapter three
Bookmarks

Chain Link & Key Pattern Bookmark

This design is made up of two different elements. The border is a very basic key pattern design such as is found on a 5th/4th century BC bronze flagon from Eigenbilzen, Belgium. While the interlinked diamonds form an overlapping chain in a similar style to knotwork, but with a more modern look.

Stitching note

Work the centre links by using all three colours at once. As you finish each link and the thread is on the reverse side of your work, remove the thread from your needle and let it hang down. Work the next two colours in the same way and then thread your needle with the first colour again, pass it under the stitches on the reverse side of your work until you reach the starting point for the next link in that colour. Do this with each colour in turn, but be careful not to stitch over the loose ends of each thread whilst working a different colour or you will not be able to weave them under the stitches neatly and you will end up with little lumps and bumps which may show through to the front of your work.

Skill level Experienced
Completion time Two to three days
Fabric 2in (5cm) Aida Band, 14-count, white edged with blue, 11in (27.5cm) long
Stitch count 22 x 118
Design size 1⅝ x 8¼in (4 x 21cm)

Threads required

		Anchor	DMC	Madeira	Amount
	Sky blue, light	130	809	0909	5ft 5in (1m 63cm)
	Sky blue, medium	131	798*	0911	5ft 7in (1m 68cm)
	Sky blue, dark	132	798*	0912	4ft 11in (1m 48cm)

*DMC conversions from Anchor are the same in these two threads

Face pattern bookmark

This design is inspired by the human face masks from 5th/4th century BC France and Germany. These masks were not always intended to be actual faces, but were often patterns that, if looked at in a certain way, gave the appearance of a face. They might be made up of scrolls, lozenges, circles, spirals and palmettes. These were sometimes used as a single pattern type or as combinations.

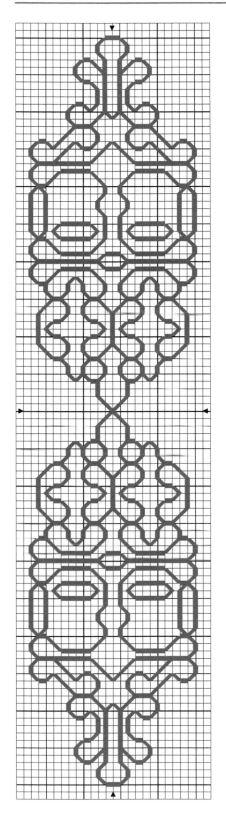

Skill level Beginner

Completion time One to two days

Fabric 2in (5cm) Aida Band, 14-count, black, 10in (25cm) long

Stitch count 22 × 100

Design size $1^5/8 \times 7^1/8$in (4×18cm)

Threads required

		Anchor	DMC	Madeira	Amount
▨	Jade, light	208	563	1207	5ft 10in (1m 75cm)

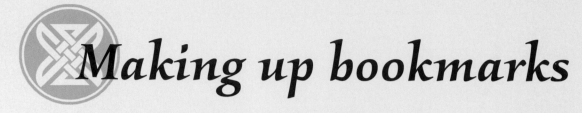

Making up bookmarks

If your work needs washing, follow the instructions that are given in Chapter 2 (see page 30). If not, just follow the instructions for pressing (see page 31).

FROM AIDA BANDS

Tools and materials
Felt, 2in (5cm) × length of design
Iron-on hemming webbing × 3 lengths, length of design
Embroidery scissors
Fabric stiffener
Tapestry needle
Towel
Iron

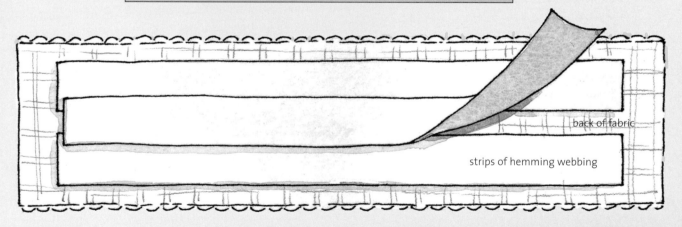

back of fabric

strips of hemming webbing

Fig 3.1 Applying the three lengths of hemming webbing

Place your work face down on a clean towel and lay the three lengths of hemming webbing side by side along the length of the design, on the reverse side of the fabric. It doesn't matter if these lengths overlap each other, but they musn't go past the edge of the design area; this includes the unsewn area at the top and bottom of the band. Lay the felt on top, taking care not to disturb the hemming webbing as you do so.

With your iron on a medium-hot setting, press it repeatedly onto the assembled layers. Do not drag it over the felt or you may cause it to pucker and bond with the Aida with creases set in it. It doesn't take very long for the fabrics to fuse, but it is quite easy to miss a small area, so it is essential that you check they have fused over their entire area before you continue. If they have, switch off your iron and leave it to cool, and move your Aida band to a clean, firm surface.

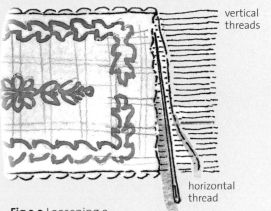

vertical threads

horizontal thread

Fig 3.2 Loosening a thread with the sharp end of a tapestry needle

Using embroidery scissors, carefully trim back any excess felt from the scalloped edges of the band. Do this a little at a time to avoid cutting through the scalloped edging itself. When you have finished trimming the sides, trim across the top and bottom edges, but don't cut too closely to the design or you may find that the stitching shows under the edge.

Finishing off

Now is the time to decide how to finish the ends off. Whatever method you choose, it is a good idea to brush a little fabric stiffener along the row of blocks just beyond the edge of the stitched area, and leave it to dry. This will help to prevent the fabric fraying into the design. You could finish off by simply cutting the Aida back to just before the row of blocks you painted with fabric stiffener. Your bookmark would then be ready to use straight away.

Working with Aida bands

Some bands have an interlocking thread running along the length of one side to prevent excessive fraying. There is no way of identifying whether your band has this until you start removing threads, but if it does, each time you reach it, your progress will be halted. Cut it back as you go, but be careful not to cut into the fringe itself.

Fringes

You may prefer to fringe your bookmark, as I have done with many of mine. This is also quite a simple procedure. The first step is to ensure that the top and bottom fringes will be the same length. To do this, count the number of holes at each end; if one end has more than the other, simply trim back the longer end until it has the same number as the shorter one. When you remove some of the horizontal threads from the band, you will find that the remaining vertical threads form a fringe. Use the point of your tapestry needle to loosen the first horizontal thread nearest the raw edge and pull it clear (see Fig 3.2). You may find that you have to remove a couple of threads that have been cut through before you reach a point where you have a continuous thread but once you do, you will be able to gently pull this until you have the length of fringe required. Be careful not to tangle the fringing threads as you work; this can cause the fabric to pucker and spoil your work. It could also lead to you removing more threads than you want to, through pulling the tangled length too hard. It is best to keep at least one row of blocks between the stitched area and the fringe – if you get any closer than this, your stitching will come undone.

When you have finished creating your fringe, cut off the threads that formed the scalloped edging as close as you can to the point where you have ended your fringing. As these threads are thicker than the vertical threads of the Aida band, they will spoil the look of the fringe even if they are the same colour. Once you have trimmed both ends, your bookmark is ready to use.

Chapter four
Coasters

Key pattern coaster

This design is a very simple key pattern that is often used in Celtic art for filling in geometrical shapes or gaps in designs.

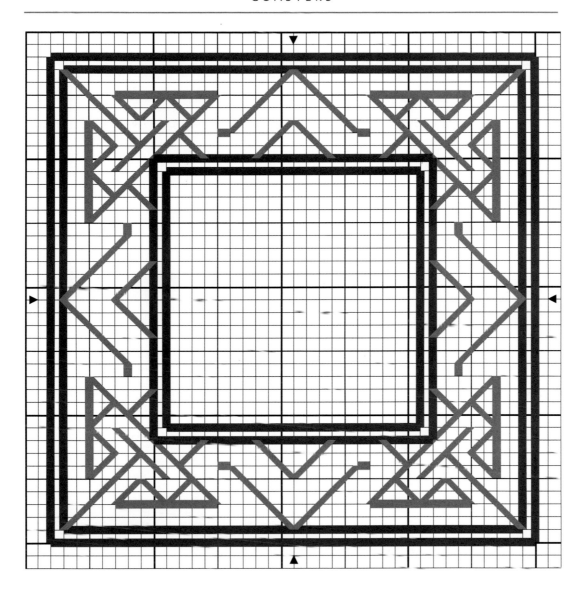

Skill level Beginner
Average completion time
One to two days
Fabric Zweigart Aida,
14-count, white, 4 x 4in
(10 x 10cm)
Stitch count 38 x 38
Design size 2³/₄ x 2³/₄in
(7 x 7cm)

Threads required

		Anchor	DMC	Madeira	Amount
	Violet, light	97	553	0711	28in (70cm)
	Violet, dark	100	327	0713	34in (85cm)

Interlinked tile coaster

This design is a modern take on Celtic art. It is made up of several hoop tiles or rounded squares that have been interlinked. Because of their shape they have two distinct meeting places. The first one is clearly where the corners meet, forming a small diamond. The second is where the bands of the squares cross over and under each other, forming a swastika pattern.

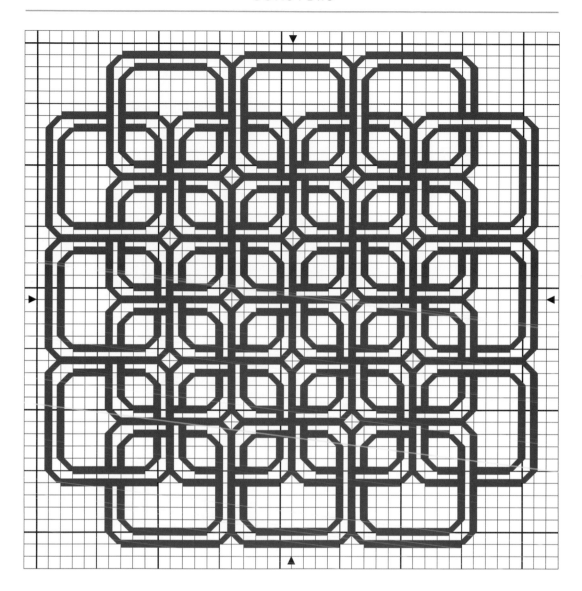

Skill level Experienced
Average completion time
Two to three days
Fabric Zweigart Aida,
14-count, cream 4 x 4in
(10 x 10cm)
Stitch count 40 x 40
Design size 2⁷/8 x 2⁷/8in
(7.5 x 7.5cm)

Threads required

		Anchor	DMC	Madeira	Amount
■	Black-brown, very dark	382	3371	2004	29ft (8.8m)

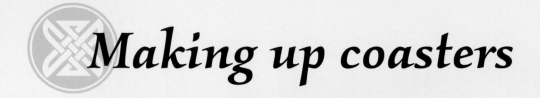 # *Making up coasters*

Tools and materials
Iron-on interfacing, 10 × 10cm (4 × 4in)
Clear acrylic coaster pack, square
Pencil or tailors' chalk
Embroidery scissors
Towel
Iron

If your work needs washing, follow the instructions given in Chapter 2 for washing and pressing (see page 30). If not, just follow the instructions for pressing.

Place your work face down on a clean towel and place the interfacing on top of it, with the slightly shiny side down, matching the corners as best you can. Fix in place by dabbing the whole surface with a medium-hot iron: if you drag the iron, you may end up with the creases fused into the layers. When you are happy that the two layers are fully fused, switch off the iron and leave it to cool.

Transfer your work to a firm surface that is clean and dry. Undo the coaster pack and spread out its contents; you should have a coaster blank, a card insert and a back plate. Using the clear plastic back plate as a pattern (this is fractionally bigger than the size of the finished piece), place it on the reverse side of your work, centre the design under it, and trace around it. Cut around your outline using embroidery scissors to ensure a sharp, crisp cut. Try your work in the recess of the coaster blank to see if it fits neatly. If it bulges, remove it and trim back a little more. Be careful not to cut too much off or gaps will show around the edge, which will spoil the finished effect.

When you are happy with the fit, place the coaster blank face down and insert your finished design (also face down) into the recess. Place the card insert on top and, finally, lay the back plate on the card. Some back plates have a right and a wrong side; if there is any moulded writing, feet or marks on the plates, make sure these face the outside of the assembled layers or the raised areas may prevent you from fixing the back plate in place. Press down hard around the edge of the plate until you are sure that it is fixed under the lugs or rim that will hold it in place.

Once fully assembled your coaster is ready to use, but please remember that it is not watertight so don't immerse it in water to wash it, simply wipe over the surface with a clean, damp cloth.

Fig 4.1
A coaster pack should contain a coaster blank, a card insert and a back plate. They are available in a range of shapes though for the patterns here you will just need square ones

Chapter five
Scented sachets

Spiral square sachet

This design is made up of several very simple spirals which, unlike the three-legged triskeles, have four legs and are often referred to as whirligigs. They may well have originated from the shape of a cross but, undoubtedly, were related to the swastika pattern and were quite common throughout the Celtic era.

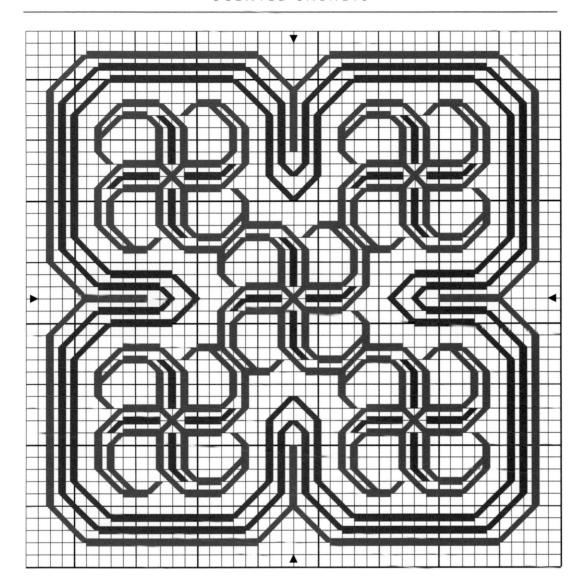

Skill level Beginner
Completion time One to two days
Fabric Zweigart Aida, 14-count, ivory, 4 x 4in (10 x 10cm)
Stitch count 40 x 40
Design size 2⅞ x 2⅞in (7.5 x 7.5cm)

Threads required

		Anchor	DMC	Madeira	Amount
■	Christmas Red, light	46	666	0210	52in (1m 30cm)
■	Christmas Red, medium	47	321	0509	35in (88cm)

Simple Knotwork Square Sachet

This design simplifies knotwork to its most basic form. Using a single 'ribbon' and simple loops, it crosses over itself forming the central design. This design is then repeated at the corners to form part of the border.

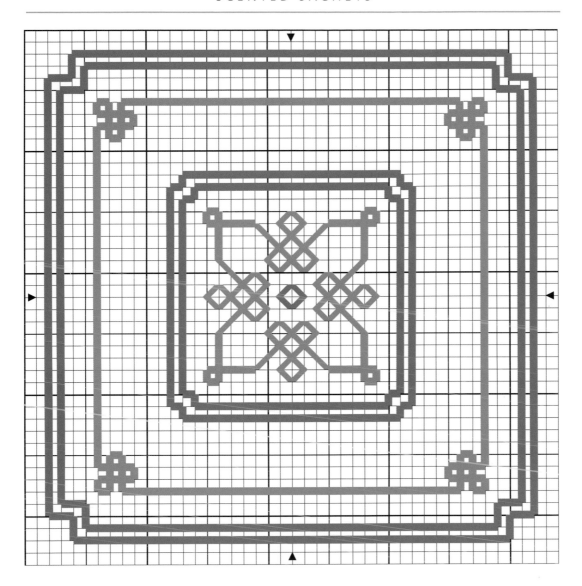

Skill level Beginner
Completion time One to two days
Fabric Zweigart Aida, 14-count, cream, 4 x 4in (10 x 10cm)
Stitch count 40 x 40
Design size 2⅞ x 2⅞in (7.5 x 7.5cm)

Threads required

		Anchor	DMC	Madeira	Amount
	Golden Brown, dark	1003	3776	0307	24in (60cm)
	Golden Brown, very dark	1004	920	0312	35in (88cm)

Making up square sachets

Count the number of unstitched holes around the design area and trim the fabric back where necessary, so that all four sides are even. Cut your backing Aida to the same size. Paint a little fabric stiffener along the row of blocks nearest the raw edge on all sides of both pieces of fabric (design and backing) and leave to dry for about one hour.

Flowers sachet

Pin a length of braid along each side of both pieces of Aida, leaving an extra 1½in (3.75cm) overhanging at each end, and ensuring that you have covered the last two blocks along the edge of the fabric. Using running stitch and a suitably coloured thread, stitch the braid in place. Next, align your two Aida pieces, with the design facing out, then pin the outer edges of the braid strips along three sides together. Use a tiny running stitch to close these three sides, then fill the sachet with your chosen pot-pourri and stitch up the final side of the braid. Form the tassels following the instructions given in Chapter 2 (see page 32) and your sachet will be ready for display.

If you want to renew the pot-pourri at a later date, carefully unpick the stitching along one edge of the braid, shake out the old pot-pourri, refill, then stitch up the braid again; make sure you fasten off any loose ends of the old stitching too.

Quad-knot drawstring sachet

The centrepiece of this design was inspired by a drawing in Courtney Davis's book, *Knotwork and Spirals* (Cassell Illustrated). This particular drawing was derived from carvings on the Ulbster Stone in Scotland.

Skill level Intermediate
Completion time Three to four days
Fabric Zweigart Aida, 14-count, cream, 7¹/₂ x 8in (18.75 x 20cm), 2 pieces
Stitch count 80 x 83
Design size 5³/₄ x 5⁷/₈in (14.5 x 15cm)

Threads required

		Anchor	DMC	Madeira	Amount
	Antique turquoise, very dark	1076	3810	1206	23ft (6m 90cm)

Scroll-etched knot drawstring sachet

This design is inspired by the scroll and tendril patterns often etched on to scabbards and razors such as those from Hungary, Switzerland, Serbia, Slovakia and Croatia in the 3rd/2nd centuries BC.

Skill level Beginner
Completion time Three to
four days
Fabric Zweigart Aida,
14-count, light grey, 5½ x6½in
(13.75 x 16.25cm), 2 pieces
Stitch count 56 x 59
Design size 4 x 4¼in
(10 x 11cm)

Threads required

		Anchor	DMC	Madeira	Amount
■	Lavender, medium dark	110	208	0804	13ft (3m 90cm)

Making up drawstring sachets

Tools and materials
12in (30cm) of ⅛in (0.3cm) wide satin ribbon, two lengths
12in (30cm) of ¼in (0.7cm) wide satin ribbon, two lengths
Two lengths of hemming webbing 1in (2.5cm) shorter than
the width of the Aida
30in (75cm) bias binding
Lavender or other dry pot-pourri
Sharp sewing needle
Sewing cotton to match Aida
Embroidery scissors
Pins

Stitching note

If you don't want to make these sachets up as drawstring bags, but would prefer to do them as square sachets simply leave off the border and adjust the size of the aida to suit. Also, if you would like a softer, more relaxed type of drawstring sachet consider using evenweave instead of Aida. However, be careful when stitching on this that you don't pull the stitches too tight.

If your work needs washing, follow the instructions given in Chapter 2 for washing and pressing (see page 30). If not, just follow the instructions for pressing.

Check that you have the same number of holes on each side beyond the edge of the design on each of the design pieces. If not, trim back to match the number on the narrowest side. Repeat this process so that both bottom edges are the same distance from the bottom edge of the stitching and then match the top edges to each other in the same manner. Cut two lengths of bias binding so that they are about ½in (1.25cm) shorter than the width of the Aida. With the reverse side of the design facing, pin this horizontally between the top stitching of the main area of design and the bottom stitching of the border. Turn the raw ends under and stitch in place to form a tunnel, open at both ends. Make sure that these ends are far enough away from the edges of the Aida so that they won't get stitched over when you make your side seams. Repeat this process for the other design piece.

Pin the two right sides together along both sides and the bottom edge, but leaving the top edge open. Stitch with a seam allowance of ⅜in (1cm) or so that the outer edges of the borders meet, but do not overlap, whichever is more suitable. This will then give the appearance of a continuous border right around the top of the sachet when it is finished. Now cut two pieces of bias binding long enough to go from the bottom corner of the side seams right up to the top edge of the stitched border; allow just a little extra to fold under to stop the raw ends from fraying. Fold one of these in half lengthwise and pin it over the raw edge of the Aida along the whole length of the seam, this will prevent the Aida from fraying. Do the same with the remaining piece of bias binding along the other seam.

Fold down the raw edge of the Aida at the top a couple of blocks or so above the top of the stitched border, but making sure that it doesn't come down lower than the bias binding tunnel. Take one length of hemming webbing and slide this under the edge of the fabric from one side-seam to the other, making sure that it comes right down to the edge of the Aida but not beyond it. Iron this into place using a medium-hot iron. Check that it has fused the two layers together properly, then repeat the process for the other side of the sachet. Once you are satisfied that both sides are secure, switch off the iron and leave it to cool.

Take one length of ⅛in (0.3cm) wide satin ribbon and one length of ¼in (0.7cm) wide satin ribbon, put them together and thread them through the tunnel made by the bias binding on one side of the sachet. Ensure that you don't pull them right through or you will lose the ends and won't be able to pull the sachet tight. Repeat this process with the other two pieces of ribbon on the other side of the sachet.

Fill the sachet with lavender or your chosen dry pot-pourri to just below the bottom edge of the bias binding. Keeping the sachet upright so as not to spill any of its contents, take hold of the four ends of ribbon and gently pull upwards to tighten the neck of the sachet. You may have to ease the Aida along in order to help with the gathering process, as the fabric is quite stiff and can sometimes be difficult to crush.

Once you have the sachet tight enough to stop the lavender/pot-pourri from falling out, tie the ends of the ribbons together in one big knot. You will need to tie a couple of knots, one over the other, to ensure that they won't come undone. If you don't intend to hang the sachet up, you can simply let the ends of the ribbons hang down like I have done; however, if you would like to hang it up you will need to tie a secure knot in the ends of the ribbons to form a loop.

Chapter six
Clutch purse

# Clutch purse

This design is made up of a central boss similar to that found on Celtic shields, surrounded by octagonal shaping which is then squared off by quarter panels of key pattern.

A black and white version of this chart which can be enlarged on a photocopier for easier working, can be found on page 123

Skill level Intermediate
Completion time Six weeks
Fabric Zweigart Aida, 14-count, black, 13 x 16in (32.5 x 40cm)
Stitch count 150 x 188
Design size 10³/₄ x 13³/₈in (10 x 6.88cm)

Threads required

		Anchor	DMC	Madeira	Amount
	Turquoise, very light	185	964	1112	699in (17m 47.5cm)
	Turquoise, very dark	189	3812	1203	928in (23m 20cm)

Making up the clutch purse

Tools and materials

Felt, 11¾ x 14in (29.5 x 35cm)

Iron-on bonding web in sheet form, 11¾ x 14in (29.5 x 35cm), two pieces

Lining fabric (cotton or satin), 11¾ x 14in (29.5 x 35cm)

Hemming webbing, 11½in (28.75cm) long

Metal shield-type button

4in (10cm) of ¼in (0.7cm) wide black satin ribbon

39in (1m) of 1⅜in (3.5cm) wide black satin ribbon

Sharp sewing needle

Sewing cotton to match Aida

Embroidery scissors

Pins

If your work needs washing, follow the washing and pressing instructions given in Chapter 2 (see page 30). If not, just follow the instructions for pressing.

With the right side facing upwards, trim back the Aida so that you have ½in (1.2cm) or seven holes between the last row of stitches and the edge of the fabric on all sides. To shape the front flap, take a pin and position it vertically into the row of holes running down towards the edge of the Aida on the left-hand side of the central section of the design, at the point where the horizontal stitching starts to slope diagonally downwards. Do the same for the right-hand side. Now take another pin and position it horizontally into the row of holes running across to the left-hand edge of the Aida at the point where the stitching finishes sloping diagonally downwards. Again, do the same for the right-hand side. These lines of holes marked with the pins show the points at which your cuts must end.

Cut along the line of holes that run horizontally towards the vertically placed pins ½in (1.2cm) or seven holes from the last row of horizontal stitching on both sides of the central section of the design. Be very careful not to cut beyond the vertical pins. Now cut along the line of holes that run vertically towards the horizontally placed pins ½in (1.2cm) or seven holes from the last row of vertical stitching on both sides of the central section of the design. Again, do not cut beyond the horizontal pins. Remove the pins and cut diagonally between the points where the horizontal and vertical cuts end, make sure that you follow the same angle as the diagonal stitching. Do this for both sides. You should have two cut-out rectangles each with one corner missing, which you can now discard.

Fold a clean, dry towel and place this on your ironing board, lay your work face-down on top of the towel. Lay the one piece of iron-on bonding sheet on top of this, making sure that you have the paper side facing up and that it is lined up properly with the side edges, but is about ½in (1.2cm) above the non-shaped bottom edge of the Aida and not beyond or you will end up bonding your work to the towel. With your iron set to a medium-hot setting carefully iron the bonding sheet in place, avoid ironing the areas where you have cut out the Aida, leave it to cool for a few seconds and then peel off the backing paper and cut off the excess bonding webbing from the shaped areas. Take the piece of felt and lay it on top of your work, again making sure that it lines up properly with the side edges and is about ½in (1.2cm) above the non-shaped bottom edge of the Aida. Iron in place carefully; use a dabbing motion rather than dragging the iron over the felt, working from the centre outwards to ensure that the felt doesn't move or crease.

Take the last piece of iron-on bonding sheet and lay it on top of the felt, make sure that you have the side edges lined up as before and that you have lined up the bottom edge as before, and follow the same procedure again. Now lay the cotton or satin lining fabric in place with the right side facing upwards (if you are using satin lining fabric you will need to turn the temperature down on your iron to a silk setting), making sure it lines up with the area covered by the bonding sheet. Iron in place, working from the centre outwards to make sure that it doesn't wrinkle or crease. Cut around the shaping for the front flap to remove the unwanted pieces of felt and lining fabric.

Now fold down the non-shaped edge of the Aida at a point about two blocks above the last row of stitching so that it covers the raw edges of the felt and lining fabric. Pin down temporarily at the edges and position the length of hemming webbing under the Aida, making sure it comes right down to the raw edge of the Aida but not beyond. Iron in place in the same manner as you did with the sheet bonding webbing, starting at the centre point and working outwards towards both seams in order to get a smooth finish. When you are satisfied that the Aida is securely fused, switch your iron off and leave it to cool.

Fold the non-shaped edge of your work upwards horizontally along the gap between the two rows of stitching so that you now have two squares of the design facing you. Pin the edges together at both sides and stitch with a seam allowance of ⅜in (1cm), to form an envelope. Take the length of ¼in (0.7cm) wide ribbon and fold it in half, pin this to the reverse side of the front flap to form a loop, but so that the raw ends do not extend beyond the point where the design stitching begins on the right side and that the two outer edges line up vertically with the vertical stitching on the front, then stitch in place.

Take the length of 1⅜in (3.5cm) wide ribbon and cut off two lengths 12in (30cm) long. Fold one in half lengthwise and fold one raw end under. Starting at the bottom edge of one of the sides, pin this in position so that it covers the raw edges of the fabric. Carry on past the point where the seam finishes until you reach the top corner of the flap. Fold the ribbon so that it forms a neat corner, and then continue horizontally until you reach the point where the Aida starts to slope. Fold the raw end under (you may need to trim a little off the end of the ribbon to form a neat fold) and then stitch in place, making sure that you stitch through the ribbon on both sides.

Now cut two pieces of 1⅜in (3.5cm) ribbon 2in (5cm) long. Again, fold the raw ends under and fold in half lengthwise, then pin this along the sloping edges of the front flap. You will have to angle the folds at both ends so that you can be sure that each piece of ribbon covers the place where the previous ribbon ended and that it will be covered by the start of the next piece. Stitch these pieces in place. Finally, cut a length of 1⅜in (3.5cm) wide ribbon 6¾in (17cm) long, fold this in half crosswise to find the centre and mark this point with a pin. Match this with the central point of the squared edge of the front flap, fold in half lengthwise as

Style note

If you can get hold of satin bias binding in a width no narrower than 1⅛in (3cm) you will be able to fold this over the raw edges and so avoid having to keep cutting it into sections. If you prefer to use braid, choose a lightweight, woven braid no narrower that 1¼in (3.2cm). Again, there should be no need to keep cutting it into sections as the weave of the braid should allow it to bend more easily. Alternatively you could gather the 1⅜in (3.5cm) ribbon so that it forms a ruched effect. This will make it easier to apply to the shaped front flap, however, you will need at least a third extra in length to do this satisfactorily.

before and pin in place. Fold the ribbon so that it forms neat corners, then continue down both sides until you reach the point where the previous ribbon ended. Fold the raw ends under as before, cutting off any excess as required, but make sure that you leave sufficient to angle the folds so that you can cover the point where the previous pieces of ribbon finished. Stitch in place, ensuring that you stitch through both sides of the ribbon.

Now fold the loop created by the ¼in (0.7cm) wide ribbon over the reverse side of the ribbon binding so that the loop is now beyond the edge of the front flap and stitch along it lengthwise in both places from the folded end to the folded edge of the ribbon binding. Fold the front flap down along the gap between the two lines of horizontal stitching so that you have two full squares of design on the back of the purse and mark with a pin the position where you will want to place the button in the apex of the loop. Stitch the button in place then loop the ribbon around it. You will probably need to press along the fold of the front flap to make it stay in place as it will initially have a tendency to spring up, but pressing should prevent this happening. Your purse is now ready to use.

Chapter seven

Purse and bag set

# *Small purse*

This design is inspired by a portion of border found on a flagon from Reinheim, Germany during the 4th century BC.

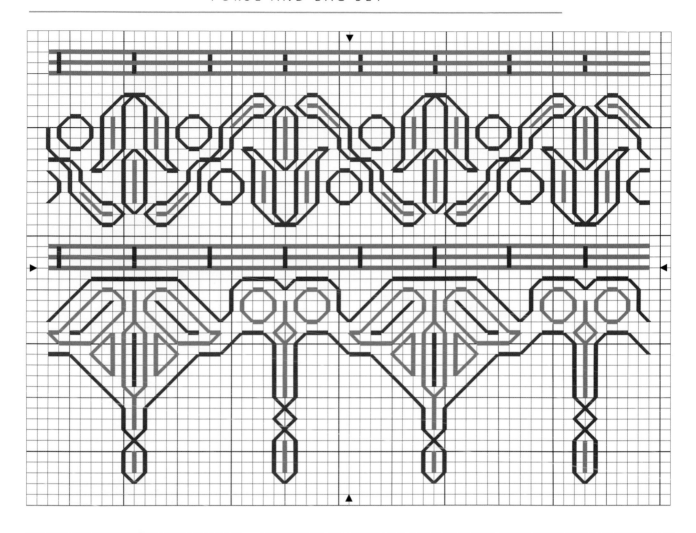

Skill level Intermediate
Completion time One week
Fabric Zweigart Aida, 14-count, sage green, 6 x 6in
(15 x 15cm), two pieces
Stitch count 56 x 38
Design size 4 x 2³/₄in
(10 x 6.88cm)

Threads required

		Anchor	DMC	Madeira	Amount
	Dusty plum, ultra very dark	72	814	0601	52¹/₂in (1m 32cm)
	Plum, medium	76	3687	0604	45in (1m 12.5cm)

Hippi bag

This design uses the same border as the small purse; however, the pattern panels are inspired by similar panels on a flagon from Waldalgesheim, Germany during the 4th century BC.

Skill level Intermediate
Completion time Three months
Fabric Zweigart Aida, 14-count, sage green, 14 x 20in (35 x 50cm), two pieces
Stitch count 168 x 227
Design size 12 x 16¼in (30 x 40.63cm)

Threads required

		Anchor	DMC	Madeira	Amount
	Dusty plum, ultra very dark	72	814	0601	82ft (24m 95cm)
	Plum, medium	76	3687	0604	27ft (8m 30cm)
	Plum, very dark	78	3685	0705	92.5ft (28m 20cm)

A black and white version of this chart,
which can be enlarged on a photocopier for
easier working, can be found on page 134

Making up small purse

> **Tools and materials**
> Felt, 6 x 5in (15 x 12.5cm), two pieces
> Iron-on bonding web in sheet form, 6 x 5in (15 x 12.5cm),
> 4 pieces
> Cotton lining fabric, 6 x 5in (15 x 12.5cm), 2 pieces
> 2 lengths of hemming webbing, 5in (12.5cm) long
> 14in (35cm) bias binding
> Velcro, 5½in (13.75cm)
> Sharp sewing needle
> Sewing cotton to match Aida
> Embroidery scissors
> Pins

If your work needs washing, follow the washing and pressing instructions given in Chapter 2 (see page 30). If not, just follow the instructions for pressing.

Fold a clean, dry towel and place this on your ironing board, then lay both pieces of your work face down on top of the towel. Lay one piece of iron-on bonding sheet on top of each of them, making sure that you have the paper side facing up and that it is lined up properly with the bottom and side edges of the Aida and not beyond or you will end up bonding your work to the towel. With your iron set to a medium-hot setting carefully iron the bonding sheet in place, leave it to cool for a few seconds and then peel off the backing paper. Now take the two pieces of felt and lay one on top of each piece of your work, again making sure that it lines up properly with the bottom and side edges of the Aida. Iron in place carefully; use a dabbing motion rather than dragging the iron over the felt, working from the centre outwards to ensure that the felt doesn't move or crease.

Take the last two pieces of iron-on bonding sheet and lay one over the top of each layer of felt, make sure that you have the bottom and side edges lined up as before and follow the same procedure again. Now lay the cotton lining fabric in place with the right side facing upwards; make sure it lines up with the area covered by the bonding sheet. Iron in place, working from the centre outwards to make sure that it doesn't wrinkle or crease.

Turn your work over so that you now have the design side facing upwards. Separate the two halves of the Velcro, pin one half along the top edge of one piece of the design and the other half along the top edge of the other piece. Leave approximately two blocks above the last of the stitching, then stitch in place along both edges of the Velcro.

Now lay one piece of your work on top of the other with the right sides of the design together, positioning the top edges so that the Velcro matches up correctly. Pin the sides and bottom edges together and stitch with a seam allowance of ⅜in (1cm). Trim back any excess felt or cotton lining fabric that may be protruding over the edge of the Aida. Now take the length of bias binding, fold it in half lengthwise and starting just under the Velcro pin it along the seam stitching so that it covers the raw edges of the fabric working right around to the top on the other side and finishing just below the Velcro again. Remember to turn the raw ends of the bias binding under at both ends so that it won't fray itself, then stitch in place, ensuring that you stitch through both sides.

Separate the Velcro and fold the top edge down on one side so that the Velcro is now covering the top edge of the lining fabric and secure temporarily in the centre with a pin. Slip one length of hemming webbing under the edge at the seam end and smooth out in the direction of the pin. Make sure that it comes down to the edge of the Aida/Velcro, but not beyond. Iron in place in the same manner as you did with the bonding sheet, working from the seam edge towards the pin. Don't go too close to the pin at this point or you might iron a crease into the hemming webbing and try not to linger too long in one place or you might melt the Velcro.

Once you are satisfied that the Aida has fused properly to the lining fabric along this part, remove the pin and smooth the hemming webbing out in the direction of the other seam. Again, make sure that it lines up with the edge of the Aida/Velcro. Iron in place in the same manner as before until you have correctly fused the two layers. Do the same with the other side of the Velcro, then turn off the iron and leave to cool.

Now turn your work so that you have the right side facing out, pushing any fabric that has bunched up in the bottom corners outwards. Match up the Velcro and smooth out the Aida along the seam to make a neat rectangle. Your purse is now ready to use.

Style note

If you want to shape the bottom of the purse like I did, follow the instructions to fuse all the layers together, then use the bottom of a clean tin or similar round object. Position this so that it comes up the side and bottom edges, then draw around the circular shape between the side and the bottom edges. Cut back to this line on both sides of the purse, and then continue with the instructions for the seams.

Making up the hippi bag

Tools and materials

100in (2m 50cm) ¼in (0.6cm) round braid, three lengths

two lengths of hemming webbing, 13in (32.5cm) long

50in (1m 25cm) bias binding

Cotton lining fabric, 14 x 19in (35 x 47.5cm), two pieces

Lightweight wadding, 14 x 19in (35 x 47.5cm), two pieces

Sharp sewing needle

Sewing cotton to match Aida

Embroidery scissors

Pins

If your work needs washing, follow the washing and pressing instructions given in Chapter 2 (see page 30). If not, just follow the instructions for pressing.

Check that you have the same number of holes on each side beyond the edge of the design on each of the design pieces; if not, trim back to match the number on the narrowest side. Repeat this process so that both bottom edges are the same distance from the bottom edge of the stitching and then match the top edges to each other in the same manner.

Place the two right sides of the design together and pin in place temporarily, making sure that the side edges of the borders match up. Lay one of the pieces of wadding on top of the reverse side of the design and then lay the cotton lining fabric on top of this, making sure that you have the right side facing up. Match these to the bottom edge of the Aida so that you have about 1in (2.5cm) of Aida showing above the top edges. Pin these layers together at the sides, but be careful not to disturb the position of the design. Turn the whole thing over and repeat the last stage with the other piece of wadding and the cotton lining fabric, again making sure that the position of the design does not change. Now smooth the layers downwards to ensure that there are no creases or puckering and pin the bottom edges together.

Stitch around these three sides with a seam allowance of ⅜in (1cm). If you are using a sewing machine try not to let it run away with you as the layers of fabric and wadding can sometimes move against each other while you are stitching and this will alter their final position and can lead to a distortion of the bag.

Trim back any excess wadding that may have squeezed out beyond the edge of the Aida and lining fabric during the stitching process. Then take the bias binding and, folding it in half lengthwise as you go, pin it over the raw edges of the fabric starting at the top of the lining fabric and continuing right around until you reach the top of the lining fabric again on the other side. Remember to fold the raw ends of the bias binding under at the start and finish points so that it does not fray and stitch it in place. Make sure that you stitch through both sides of the binding securely.

Keeping the bag inside out, fold down the raw edge of the Aida at the top just above the top of the stitching so that it is now covering the top edge of the lining fabric, and temporarily secure with a pin. Slip one length of hemming webbing under the edge at the seam end and smooth out in the direction of the pin. Make sure that it comes right down to the edge of the Aida, but not beyond. Iron in place in the same manner as you did with the bonding sheet, working from the seam edge towards the pin. Don't go too close to the pin at this point or you might iron a crease into the hemming webbing.

Once you are satisfied that the Aida has fused to the lining fabric along this part, remove the pin and smooth the hemming webbing out in the direction of the other seam. Again, make sure that it lines up with the edge of the Aida. Iron in place in the same manner as before until you have correctly fused the two layers. Do the same with the other side of the top of the Aida, then turn off the iron and leave to cool. Now turn your work so that you have the right side facing out, pushing any fabric that has bunched up in the bottom corners outwards.

To make the strap take the three lengths of braid and fold each one in half, marking the centre point with a pin. Secure them together at either side of this point with a few small stitches through the sides so that you have a flat spot about ½in (1.2cm) wide. Temporarily fix this point to something sturdy, such as an ironing board, or get someone to hold it, and then plait the three strands together. Try to keep the plaiting as even as possible and stop 3in (7.5cm) from the end of the braids. Temporarily secure them together at this point with some

thread to stop them from unravelling themselves. Repeat the plaiting process with the braids on the other side of the flat spot and temporarily secure again in the same manner.

Pin the plaited braid to the side seam of the bag, matching up the point where you finished plaiting to the bottom corner of the bag and work upwards until you reach the top edge. Repeat this process on the other side seam, making sure that you avoid getting any twists in the strap. Hand-stitch in place trying to keep the centre of the plait level with the seam. You will also need to stitch not only the centre of the braid in place but the two outer edges too as this will spread the tension on the strap when the bag is in use and also add to the security of the strap itself.

Once you have finished stitching the strap in place make the two tassels at the bottom of the bag. Follow the instructions in Chapter 2 (see page 32). Your bag is now ready to use.

Chapter eight
Pencil cases

Interlaced pencil case

This design is a squared-off form of knotwork using four 'ribbons'. To show the patterns formed by each 'ribbon', four different coloured infills have been used. A simple rope pattern has been used as a frame.

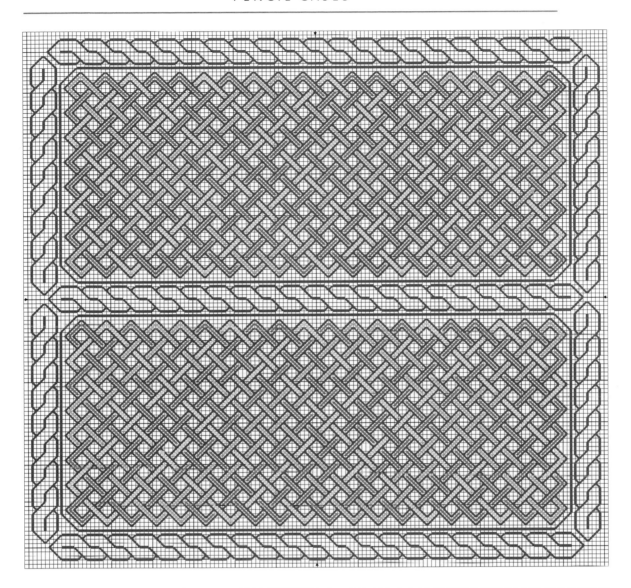

Skill level Intermediate
Completion time
Two to three weeks
Fabric Zweigart Aida,
14-count, black, 13 x 11in
(32.5 x 27.5cm)
Stitch count 138 x 126
Design size 9⅞ x 9in
(25 x 22.5cm)

Threads required

		Anchor	DMC	Madeira	Amount
	Peach, ultra very dark	13	817	0211	81ft (24m 30cm)
	Peach, dark	10	351	0214	5ft 9in (1m 73cm)
	Peach, light	8	3824	0304*	5ft 9in (1m 73cm)
	Peach, very light	6	353	0304*	5ft 9in (1m 73cm)
	Peach, very dark	11	3705	0213	5ft 9in (1m 73cm)

*Madeira conversions from Anchor are the same in these two threads

Chain and key pattern tile pencil case

Using a single ribbon to form a simple chain of knotwork and overlaying it with a smaller version in a different colour gives this design a rich border (to make it look even more lavish you could use very fine metallic braid for the top chain). The centre is then filled with little tiles of key pattern using tiny squares to represent the circles and dots often used in a lot of Celtic designs for pottery and metalwork.

A black and white version of this chart, which can be enlarged on a photocopier for easier working, can be found on page 135

Skill level Intermediate
Completion time Two weeks
Fabric Zweigart Aida, 14 count, dark green, 10½ x 12in (26.25 x 30cm)
Stitch count 107 x 123
Design size 7⅝ x 8¾in (19.5 x 22cm)

Threads required

		Anchor	DMC	Madeira	Amount
	Burnt orange, medium	302	743	0114	32ft 5in (9m 73cm)
	Burnt orange, very dark	304	741	0202	42ft 4in (13m)

Making up pencil cases

Tools and materials

Interlaced pencil case
Piece of black felt, 13 x 11in (32.5 x 27.5cm)
Two pieces of Iron-on bonding web in sheet form,
one the same size as felt and one the same
size as the lining fabric
Piece of cotton lining fabric, 13 x 10in (32.5 x 25cm)
Velcro, 10$\frac{1}{2}$in (26.25cm)
Two lengths of bias binding, 6in (15cm) long
Two lengths of hemming webbing, 10in (25cm) long

Chain and key pattern tile pencil case
Piece of green felt, 10$\frac{1}{2}$ x 12in (26.25 x 30cm)
Two pieces of iron-on bonding web in sheet form, one
the same size as felt, one the same size as the lining fabric
Piece of cotton lining fabric, 10$\frac{1}{2}$ x 11in (26.25 x 27.5cm)
Velcro, 11$\frac{1}{2}$in (28.75cmcm)
Two lengths of bias binding, 6in (15cm) long
Two lengths of hemming webbing, 11in (27.5cm) long

For both pencil cases
Sewing thread in suitable colour
Sharp sewing needle
Embroidery scissors
Towel
Iron
Pins

Stitching note

When working the border, make the outer frame first, then stitch all of the chain worked in burnt orange, very dark. Ensure that you work in the same direction all the time so that the crossover stitches are all lying in the same direction. Now overlay the smaller chain worked in burnt orange, medium, again making sure that you work in the same direction as before. When stitching the tiles, build each one individually.

If your work needs to be washed, follow the instructions given in Chapter 2 (see page 30). If not, just follow the instructions for pressing (see page 31).

Fold a clean, dry towel and place this on your ironing board, then lay your work face down on top of the towel. Check that you have the same number of holes after the last stitches of the design on each side. If not, simply trim the side that has more back to the same number as the narrower side. Lay the larger piece of iron-on bonding sheet on top of it, making sure that you have the paper side facing up and that it is lined up properly with the edges of the Aida and not beyond or you will end up bonding your work to the towel. With your iron set to a medium-hot setting carefully iron the bonding sheet in place, leave it to cool for a few seconds and then peel off the backing paper. Now take the piece of felt and lay one on top of your work, again making sure that it lines up properly with the edges of the aida. Iron in place carefully; use a dabbing motion rather than dragging the iron over the felt, working from the centre outwards to ensure that the felt doesn't move or crease.

Lay the remaining piece of iron-on bonding sheet over the top of the felt, make sure that you have the same amount of felt showing above and below it, approximately ½in (1.25cm), then follow the bonding procedure as before. Now lay the cotton lining fabric in place with the right side facing upwards, making sure it lines up with the area covered by the bonding sheet. Iron in place working from the centre outwards to make sure that it doesn't wrinkle or crease.

Turn your work over so that you now have the design side facing upwards. Separate the two halves of the Velcro, pin one half along the top edge and the other half along the bottom edge. Leave approximately two blocks above and below the last of the stitching, then stitch in place along both edges of the Velcro.

Fold your work in half horizontally, positioning the top and bottom edges so that the Velcro matches up correctly. Pin the sides together and stitch with a seam allowance of ⅜in (1cm). Trim back any excess felt or cotton lining fabric that may be protruding over the edge of the Aida. Now take one of the lengths of bias binding, fold it in half lengthwise and starting just under the Velcro pin it along the seam stitching so that it covers the raw edges of the fabrics. Remember to turn the raw ends of the bias binding under at the top and bottom so that it won't fray itself, then stitch in place making sure that you stitch both sides securely.

Separate the Velcro and fold the top edge down on one side so that the Velcro is now covering the top edge of the lining fabric, then secure it temporarily in the centre with a pin. Slip one length of hemming webbing under the edge at the seam end and smooth out in the direction of the pin. Make sure that it comes right down to the edge of the Aida/Velcro, but not beyond. Iron in place in the same way as with the bonding sheet, working from the seam edge towards the pin. Don't go too close to the pin at this point or you might iron a crease into the hemming webbing and try not to linger too long in one place or you might melt the Velcro.

Once you are satisfied that the Aida has fused to the lining fabric along this part, remove the pin and smooth the hemming webbing out in the direction of the other seam. Again, make sure that it lines up with the edge of the Aida/Velcro. Iron it in place in the same manner as before until you have correctly fused the two layers. Do the same with the other side of the Velcro, then turn off the iron and leave to cool.

Now turn your work so that you have the right side facing out, pushing any fabric that has bunched up in the bottom corners outwards. Match up the Velcro and smooth out the Aida along the seam to make a neat rectangle. Your pencil case is now ready to use.

Chapter nine
Table mat

Knotwork table mat

This design is made up of different squares of knotwork that vary in complexity and distance of the crossing points. It can be worked as a whole or broken up into sections to suit different purposes.

A black and white version of this chart, which can be elarged on a photocopier for easier working, can be found on page 136

Skill level Intermediate
Completion time Two to three weeks
Fabric Zweigart Aida, 14-count, baby pink, 12 × 12in (30 × 30cm)
Stitch count 122 × 122
Design size 8³/₄ × 8³/₄in (22 × 22cm)

Threads required

		Anchor	DMC	Madeira	Amount
	Jade, medium	210	562	1312	15ft 3in (4m 22.5cm)
	Jade, light	208	563	1207	26ft 8in (8m)
	Jade, very light	206	564	1210	17ft 11in (5m 37.5cm)

Making up table mats

Tools and materials
Felt, $8^3/_4 \times 8^3/_4$in (22 × 22cm)
Iron-on bonding webbing, same size as felt
Embroidery scissors
Tapestry needle
Towel
Iron

Wash and press your work following the instructions given in Chapter 2 (see page 30), then trim the fabric as necessary to ensure that you have the same number of holes around each side of the design.

Fold a clean, dry towel and place this on your ironing board, lay your work face down on top of this. Lay the iron-on bonding sheet on top, make sure that you have the paper side facing up and that it is lined up properly with the edges of the design and not more than one block beyond it, or you will glue the treads of the Aida together and you won't be able to fringe it properly. With your iron set to a medium-hot setting, carefully iron the bonding sheet in place, leave it to cool for a few seconds and then peel off the backing paper. Now take the piece oaf felt and lay it on top of your work, smooth out any creases or wrinkles, then check that it is still lined up with the edges of the design. If it has moved even a little, reposition it and smooth out any creases as before. Iron in place carefully; use a dabbing motion rather than dragging the iron over the felt, working from the centre outwards to ensure that the felt doesn't move or get creased. Once you are sure that it is properly fused, switch off your iron and leave it to cool.

Transfer your work to a clean, firm surface. It is now time to make the fringe. To do this, remove each of the horizontal threads from the outer edges of the fabric until you are one block away from the design; the remaining vertical threads will form the fringe (see page 44). Don't try to remove too many threads at the same time as this will cause them to tangle and you will distort the fabric as you pull. The best method is to remove one or two threads at a time, easing them out gently with the point of your tapestry needle; this will enable you to smooth out any potential tangles as you go. Work on one side at a time.

Your table mat is now ready to use. To wash it, follow the instructions given in Chapter 2 (see page 30). To dry it, lay it out flat and face down on a folded towel. Untangle and straighten the fringe, then iron dry on a medium-hot, dry setting, taking care not to distort the shape of the mat as you go.

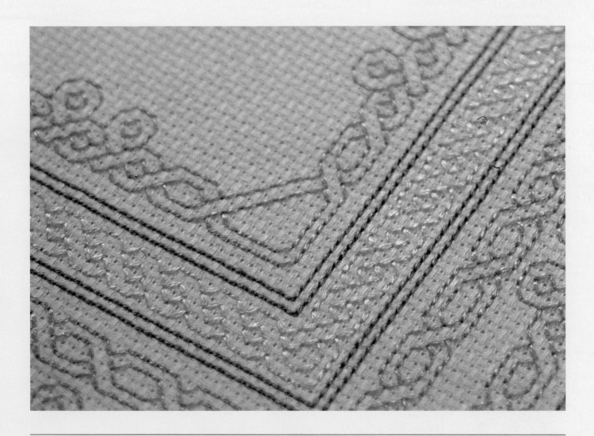

Chapter ten

Cushion and tie-backs

Key pattern cushion

This design is inspired by the Celtic cross. Individual crosses are surrounded by a maze-type key pattern broken up in places by an expanded version of the cross which also incorporates very basic knotwork.

Stitching note

Stitch all the Christmas green first then stitch your gold braid. As the gold braid has a tendency to knot very easily always pull it through the fabric slowly. When pulling it through from the back of your work it is a good idea to hold it lightly between the index finger and thumb of the hand you are not holding the needle in and let it run through them. By doing this you will smooth out any twists or loops before they can become knots. Remember, it is almost impossible to get a knot out of metallic thread once you have pulled it tight. If you want a lighter look to your metallic thread, try Kreinik very fine braid no 4.

A black and white version of this chart, which can be enlarged on a photocopier for easier working, can be found on page 137

Skill level Intermediate
Completion time Five to six weeks
Fabric Zweigart Aida, 14-count, sage green, 19 x 19in (47.5 × 47.5cm)
Stitch count 222 × 222
Design size 15⅞ × 15⅞in (40 x 40cm)

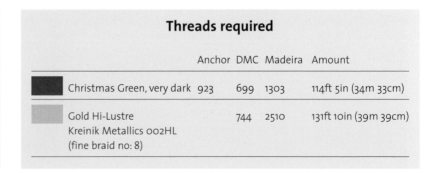

Threads required

		Anchor	DMC	Madeira	Amount
▨	Christmas Green, very dark	923	699	1303	114ft 5in (34m 33cm)
▨	Gold Hi-Lustre Kreinik Metallics 002HL (fine braid no: 8)		744	2510	131ft 10in (39m 39cm)

Key pattern curtain tie-backs

This design simply takes elements of the cushion design and arranges them in such a way as to form tie-backs for your curtains which will match your cushion.

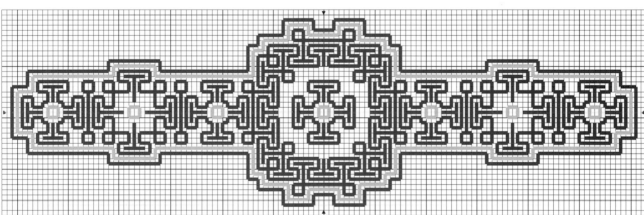

Skill level Intermediate
Completion time
One to two weeks
Fabric Zweigart Aida, 14-
count, sage green, 11$\frac{1}{2}$ x 5in
(29 x 12.5cm), two pieces
Stitch count 122 x 36
Design size 8$\frac{3}{4}$ x 2$\frac{5}{8}$in
(22 x 6.5cm)

Threads required

		Anchor	DMC	Madeira	Amount
■	Christmas Green, very dark	923	699	1303	11ft 5in (3m 43cm)
▨	Gold Hi-Lustre Kreinik Metallics 002HL (fine braid no: 8)		744	2510	14ft 5in (4m 33cm)

Making up the cushion

Tools and materials
Chosen backing fabric, in colour to complement or
contrast with design
Cushion insert, 16in (40cm), or flame-retardant polyester
toy filling
Braid (optional), 7ft 4in (2m 20cm) long
Velcro, 17in (42.5cm) long
Sewing thread in suitable colour
Sharp sewing needle and/or sewing machine
Embroidery scissors
Towel
Iron
Pins

Wash and press your work following the instructions in Chapter 2 (see page 30), then wash and press your backing fabric to ensure that it will not shrink or distort after you have made up your cushion. Trim back your design piece to 18in (45cm) square, ensuring that you have the same number of holes on all sides after the last line of stitching. Now cut your backing fabric to match your Aida piece.

I like to use Velcro to fasten this type of project as it has no sharp edges to catch on the fabric of your furniture as a zip does. If you are using polyester filling rather than a cushion insert, you will need to stitch up the final seam rather than fastening it with Velcro; follow the instructions below, but ignore the steps that involve the Velcro.

Separate the two layers of Velcro and, with the right side facing, pin one layer along one raw edge of the backing fabric. Pin the other layer to the bottom edge of the design fabric in the same way, on the design side of the Aida. Now stitch both pieces in place, making sure that you stitch over each end of the Velcro to prevent the ends from pulling out of the seams. Fold the Velcro edges over so that they are now on the reverse side of both fabrics and stitch in place, but be careful not to stitch over the design stitching.

Lay your backing fabric face up on a clean, firm surface, then place your design face down on top of it, lining up the two Velcro strips and smoothing out any creases or wrinkles. Pin the fabric pieces together along the other three sides and then stitch up the seams, by machine or by hand, leaving a ½in (1.2cm) seam allowance all around. Make sure that you have stitched over both ends of the Velcro during this process.

Turn your cushion cover inside out so that you now have the right side of the design outside. The fabric does tend to bunch up at the corners, making them slightly rounded. To remedy this, put your fingers inside the cover and push the material out to form neatly squared corners.

If you are using braid, divide it into four 22in (55cm) lengths, then tie two pieces of thread around it either side of where you want to cut to prevent it from unravelling, before you want it to. Pin one length along each side so that it covers the line of the seam and has an overhang of 2½in (6.25cm) at each end; this will form your tassel.

Hand-stitch the braid in place using a suitably coloured sewing thread and an ordinary sharp needle. Stitch into the edge of the braid that is nearest to the fabric or your stitches will show. To form the tassels, follow the instructions given in Chapter 2 (see page 32).

With the tassels made, slip your cushion insert into the cover and press the Velcro together to close it. If you are using polyester filling, simply stuff your cushion to the required firmness and stitch up the final seam. Your cushion is now ready for you to use. Remember, it is not advisable to machine-wash the cover; for the best care of your cushion cover, follow the washing instructions given in Chapter 2 (see page 30).

Making up tie-backs

Tools and materials
Two pieces of green felt, 11³/₄ x 5in (29.38 x 12.5cm)
Four pieces of iron-on bonding web in sheet form, same
size as felt
Two pieces of cotton lining fabric, same size as felt
8 x flat braid, ¹/₂in (1.2cm) wide, 19¹/₂in (50cm) long
Sewing thread in suitable colour
Sharp sewing needle
Embroidery scissors
Towel
Iron
Ruler or straight edge
Tailor's chalk or other suitable non-permanent marker
4 x 1¹/₂in (3.75cm) diameter plastic rings (optional)
Pins

If your work needs to be washed, follow the instructions given in Chapter 2 (see page 30). If not, just follow the instructions for pressing (see page 31).

Fold a clean, dry towel and place this on your ironing board. Lay the two design pieces on top of this, design side upwards. The distance from the top edge of the stitching to the top edge of the Aida needs to be 3cm (1¹/₄in); measure this and trim back as necessary, then repeat the same process for the bottom edge. The distance from the edge of the stitching at the sides to the edge of the Aida needs to be 1³/₈in (3.5cm). Again, measure this and trim back as necessary on both edges.

Turn your work over so that you now have the reverse sides of both pieces upwards and lay one piece of iron-on bonding sheet on top of each of them, making sure that you have the paper side facing up and that it is lined up properly with the edges of the Aida and not beyond or you will end up bonding your work to the towel. With your iron set to a medium-hot setting carefully iron the bonding sheet in place on both pieces, leave them to cool for a few seconds and then peel off the backing paper. Now take the two pieces of felt and lay one on top of each piece of your work, again making sure that they line up properly with the edges of the Aida. Iron in place carefully using a dabbing motion rather than dragging the iron over the felt. Work from the centre outwards so that the felt doesn't move.

Take the last two pieces of iron-on bonding sheet and lay one on top of each of the felt layers, repeat the bonding process as before and peel off the backing paper when cool. Now take the two pieces of cotton lining fabric and lay one of these on top of each piece of your work, making sure that you have the right side of the fabric facing upwards. Iron these in place, again working from the centre outwards to avoid it creasing. When you are happy that all the layers are properly fused together, switch off your iron and leave it to cool.

Now turn both pieces of work over so that you have the right sides facing upwards again, and cut the left and right sides of the Aida so that you have 1in (2.5cm) or 14 holes from the edge of the stitching to the outer edge of the Aida. Now cut the top and bottom edges so that you have ¾in (2cm) or 10 holes from the edge of the stitching to the outer edge of the Aida. Using two pins mark the line of holes which run vertically up from the last row of stitching on the outer edge of the central piece of the design on the top edge and vertically down to the bottom edge. Now do the same with the line of holes running horizontally from the outer edge of the stitching on the last section of the design on both edges. The points where the pins reach the edge of the Aida is where you will start and finish your cuts to shape the tie-backs.

Lay your ruler/straight-edge from one point to the other and draw a line with tailor's chalk or other suitable marker across the corner. Do the same for all four corners then cut along these lines.

Take two of the lengths of braid and find the centre of each, match these up to the centre of the top edge of the tie-backs on the front and reverse sides and pin in place. Work to the left and right of these points as far as the corners and pin them in place too. Stitch the braid in place using a suitable colour of sewing thread, make sure that you are stitching through the braid on both sides of the tie-back, then remove the pins.

If you are using plastic rings as I have, stop at the top corners, and position two more lengths of braid along the bottom edge of the tie-back in the same manner. Now take one of the plastic rings and fold one of the ends of the braid on the front of the tie-back through it, letting it hang down on the reverse side. Fold the opposite end of the braid from the reverse side of the tie-back through the ring and on to the front. Fold the remaining end of the braid on the front across the raw edge of the Aida and pin it in place. Do the same on the reverse side. Stitch in place using a suitable colour of sewing thread, making sure that you have turned under the raw end of the braid that crosses over the Aida and that you have thoroughly secured the braid that goes through the ring. Trim off any excess braid that hangs down past the braid that crosses over it. However, be very careful not to cut this part of the braid when you do so. Then repeat the whole process at the other end. Do this for both tie-backs.

If you are not using plastic rings, continue around the corners until you reach the centre point of the last design section. Do the same with two more lengths of braid along the bottom edge. Cross the braid over at the point where the two lengths meet at the centre of the design side; do the same on the reverse side. Stitch the braid in place using a suitable colour of sewing thread, make sure that you are stitching through the braid on both sides of the tie-back and secure the place where the braid crosses over with a couple of small stitches, then remove the pins. Working on one end of the tie-back first, put the four ends of the braids together and smooth this back towards the point where the braid crosses over until it leaves a loop approximately 1in (2.5cm) round. Secure the four pieces of braid together at this point then follow the instructions for forming a tassel given on page 32 in Chapter 2. Repeat this process at the other side of that tie-back, and then repeat the whole process for applying the braid to the other tie-back.

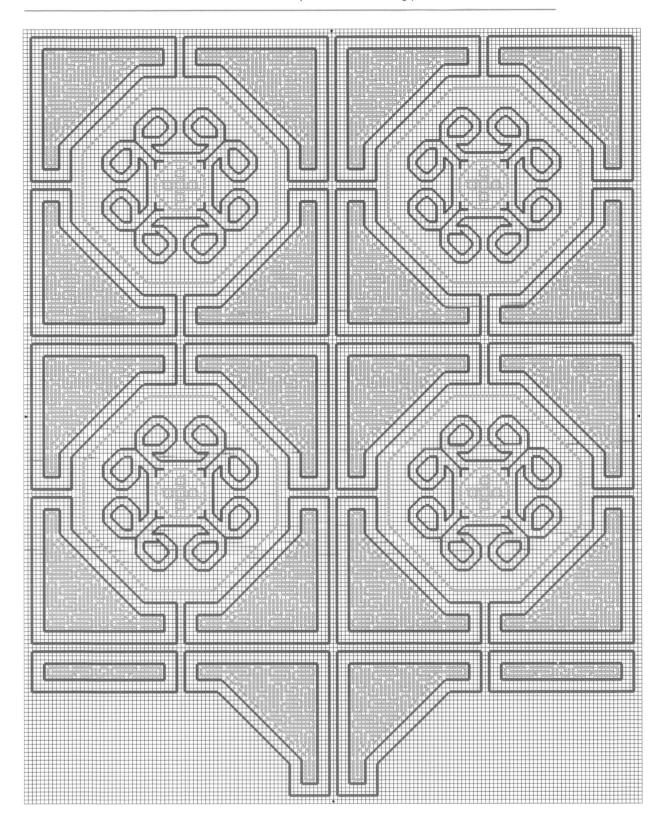

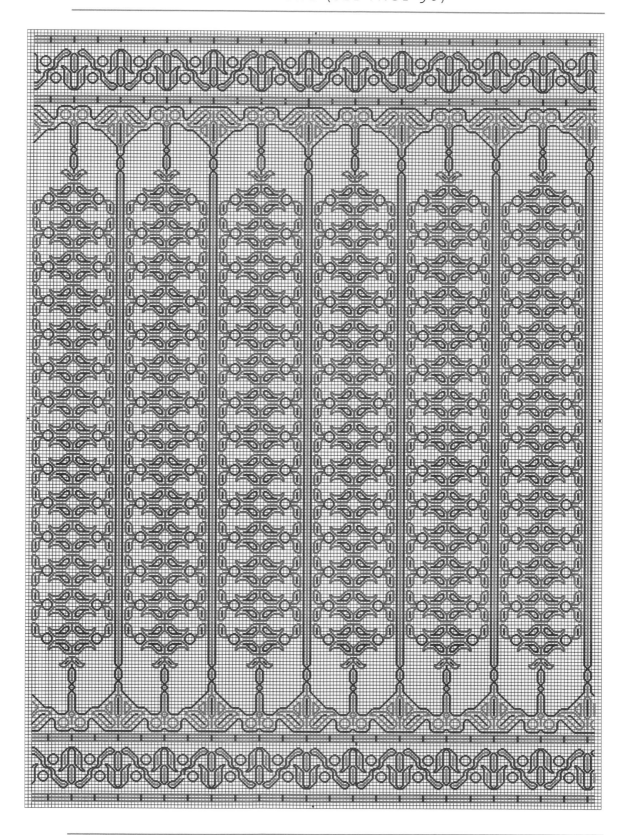

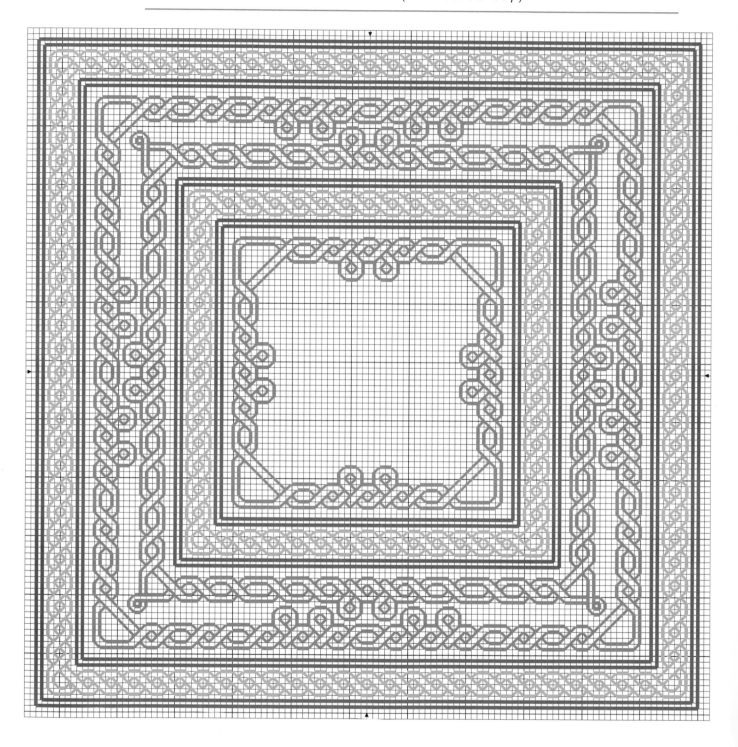

About the Author

I was taught needlework by my grandmother when I was just a little girl, as readers of my previous book *Creative Backstitch* will be aware, but since developing multiple sclerosis and a somewhat more restricted lifestyle I have expanded my skills wherever possible.

I started to develop designs that just use backstitch because I wanted to offer a different style of stitching to the world of needlework. I feel that over the last ten years or so cross stitch has rather dominated the market and, though this is good in some respects, it seems to have left very little room for any other style of stitching.

Backstitch also tends to be quick to do so although some of my backstitch designs are quite intricate and can take some time to complete, the fact that the stitching is easier and it seems to progress much more quickly means that even people new to stitching are more likely to persevere to the end.

I still enjoy doing cross-stitch designs, but these days I prefer to concentrate on my more realistic 'painting-in-stitches' style of designs that I have recently been developing. So together with my new website (www.classiccrafts.co.uk) and my continuing designing, I am looking forward to a busy, creative future for as long as my illness allows.

Index

Page numbers in bold refer to illustrations

TITLES AVAILABLE FROM
GMC Publications

BOOKS

UPHOLSTERY

Upholstery: A Complete Course (Revised Edition)   *David James*
Upholstery Restoration   *David James*
Upholstery Techniques & Projects   *David James*
Upholstery Tips and Hints   *David James*

TOYMAKING

Scrollsaw Toy Projects   *Ivor Carlyle*
Scrollsaw Toys for All Ages   *Ivor Carlyle*

DOLLS' HOUSES AND MINIATURES

1/12 Scale Character Figures for the Dolls' House   *James Carrington*
Americana in 1/12 Scale: 50 Authentic Projects
     Joanne Ogreenc & Mary Lou Santovec
The Authentic Georgian Dolls' House   *Brian Long*
A Beginners' Guide to the Dolls' House Hobby   *Jean Nisbett*
Celtic, Medieval and Tudor Wall Hangings in 1/12 Scale Needlepoint
     Sandra Whitehead
Creating Decorative Fabrics: Projects in 1/12 Scale   *Janet Storey*
Dolls' House Accessories, Fixtures and Fittings   *Andrea Barham*
Dolls' House Furniture: Easy-to-Make Projects in 1/12 Scale
     Freida Gray
Dolls' House Makeovers   *Jean Nisbett*
Dolls' House Window Treatments   *Eve Harwood*
Edwardian-Style Hand-Knitted Fashion for 1/12 Scale Dolls
     Yvonne Wakefield
How to Make Your Dolls' House Special: Fresh Ideas for Decorating
     Beryl Armstrong
Making 1/12 Scale Wicker Furniture for the Dolls' House   *Sheila Smith*
Making Miniature Chinese Rugs and Carpets   *Carol Phillipson*
Making Miniature Food and Market Stalls   *Angie Scarr*
Making Miniature Gardens   *Freida Gray*
Making Miniature Oriental Rugs & Carpets   *Meik & Ian McNaughton*
Making Miniatures: Projects for the 1/12 Scale Dolls' House
     Christiane Berridge
Making Period Dolls' House Accessories   *Andrea Barham*
Making Tudor Dolls' Houses   *Derek Rowbottom*
Making Upholstered Furniture in 1/12 Scale   *Janet Storey*
Making Victorian Dolls' House Furniture   *Patricia King*
Medieval and Tudor Needlecraft: Knights and Ladies in 1/12 Scale
     Sandra Whitehead
Miniature Bobbin Lace   *Roz Snowden*
Miniature Crochet: Projects in 1/12 Scale   *Roz Walters*
Miniature Embroidery for the Georgian Dolls' House   *Pamela Warner*
Miniature Embroidery for the Tudor and Stuart Dolls' House
     Pamela Warner
Miniature Embroidery for the 20th-Century Dolls' House
     Pamela Warner
Miniature Embroidery for the Victorian Dolls' House   *Pamela Warner*
Miniature Needlepoint Carpets   *Janet Granger*
More Miniature Oriental Rugs & Carpets   *Meik & Ian McNaughton*
Needlepoint 1/12 Scale: Design Collections for the Dolls' House
     Felicity Price

New Ideas for Miniature Bobbin Lace   *Roz Snowden*
Patchwork Quilts for the Dolls' House: 20 Projects in 1/12 Scale
     Sarah Williams
Simple Country Furniture Projects in 1/12 Scale   *Alison J. White*

CRAFTS

Bargello: A Fresh Approach to Florentine Embroidery   *Brenda Day*
Beginning Picture Marquetry   *Lawrence Threadgold*
Blackwork: A New Approach   *Brenda Day*
Celtic Cross Stitch Designs   *Carol Phillipson*
Celtic Knotwork Designs   *Sheila Sturrock*
Celtic Knotwork Handbook   *Sheila Sturrock*
Celtic Spirals and Other Designs   *Sheila Sturrock*
Celtic Spirals Handbook   *Sheila Sturrock*
Complete Pyrography   *Stephen Poole*
Creating Made-to-Measure Knitwear: A Revolutionary
     Approach to Knitwear Design   *Sylvia Wynn*
Creative Backstitch   *Helen Hall*
Creative Log-Cabin Patchwork   *Pauline Brown*
Creative Machine Knitting   *GMC Publications*
The Creative Quilter: Techniques and Projects   *Pauline Brown*
Cross-Stitch Designs from China   *Carol Phillipson*
Cross-Stitch Floral Designs   *Joanne Sanderson*
Decoration on Fabric: A Sourcebook of Ideas   *Pauline Brown*
Decorative Beaded Purses   *Enid Taylor*
Designing and Making Cards   *Glennis Gilruth*
Designs for Pyrography and Other Crafts   *Norma Gregory*
Dried Flowers: A Complete Guide   *Lindy Bird*
Exotic Textiles in Needlepoint   *Stella Knight*
Glass Engraving Pattern Book   *John Everett*
Glass Painting   *Emma Sedman*
Handcrafted Rugs   *Sandra Hardy*
Hobby Ceramics: Techniques and Projects for Beginners
     Patricia A. Waller
How to Arrange Flowers: A Japanese Approach to English Design
     Taeko Marvelly
How to Make First-Class Cards   *Debbie Brown*
An Introduction to Crewel Embroidery   *Mave Glenny*
Machine-Knitted Babywear   *Christine Eames*
Making Decorative Screens   *Amanda Howes*
Making Fabergé-Style Eggs   *Denise Hopper*
Making Fairies and Fantastical Creatures   *Julie Sharp*
Making Hand-Sewn Boxes: Techniques and Projects   *Jackie Woolsey*
Making Mini Cards, Gift Tags & Invitations   *Glennis Gilruth*
Native American Bead Weaving   *Lynne Garner*
New Ideas for Crochet: Stylish Projects for the Home   *Darsha Capaldi*
Papercraft Projects for Special Occasions   *Sine Chesterman*
Papermaking and Bookbinding: Coastal Inspirations   *Joanne Kaar*
Patchwork for Beginners   *Pauline Brown*
Pyrography Designs   *Norma Gregory*
Rose Windows for Quilters   *Angela Besley*
Silk Painting for Beginners   *Jill Clay*
Sponge Painting   *Ann Rooney*

MAGAZINES

WOODTURNING ◆ WOODCARVING ◆ FURNITURE & CABINETMAKING

THE ROUTER ◆ NEW WOODWORKING ◆ THE DOLLS' HOUSE MAGAZINE

OUTDOOR PHOTOGRAPHY ◆ BLACK & WHITE PHOTOGRAPHY

TRAVEL PHOTOGRAPHY ◆ MACHINE KNITTING NEWS

KNITTING ◆ GUILD OF MASTER CRAFTSMEN NEWS

The above represents a full list of all titles currently published or scheduled to be published.
All are available direct from the Publishers or through bookshops, newsagents and specialist retailers.
To place an order, or to obtain a complete catalogue, contact:

GMC Publications,
Castle Place, 166 High Street, Lewes,
East Sussex BN7 1XU United Kingdom
Tel: 01273 488005 Fax: 01273 402866
E-mail: pubs@thegmcgroup.com
Website: www.gmcbooks.com

Orders by credit card are accepted